The Voyage of the "Deutschland"

Paul König

(Translator: Vivien Ellis)

Alpha Editions

This edition published in 2024

ISBN : 9789364739726

Design and Setting By
Alpha Editions
www.alphaedis.com
Email - info@alphaedis.com

As per information held with us this book is in Public Domain.
This book is a reproduction of an important historical work. Alpha Editions uses the best technology to reproduce historical work in the same manner it was first published to preserve its original nature. Any marks or number seen are left intentionally to preserve its true form.

Contents

INTRODUCTION ....- 1 -
CHAPTER I HOW WE CAME TO JOIN THE "DEUTSCHLAND" AND WHAT I THOUGHT OF HER ....- 3 -
CHAPTER II THE TRIAL AND DEPARTURE ....- 7 -
CHAPTER III THE FIRST DAY AT SEA ....- 10 -
CHAPTER IV THE U-BOAT TRAP ....- 15 -
CHAPTER V A SOMERSAULT IN THE NORTH SEA ....- 19 -
CHAPTER VI OUT INTO THE OPEN ....- 24 -
CHAPTER VII IN THE ATLANTIC......................................- 27 -
CHAPTER VIII THE INFERNO ....- 36 -
CHAPTER IX AMERICA..- 39 -
CHAPTER X BALTIMORE ....- 43 -
CHAPTER XI THE DEPARTURE FROM BALTIMORE .....- 50 -
CHAPTER XII RUNNING THE BLOCKADE......................- 56 -
CHAPTER XIII THE HOMEWARD JOURNEY ....- 59 -
CHAPTER XIV THE ARRIVAL..- 65 -
CHAPTER XV THE RECEPTION OF THE " DEUTSCHLAND" BY THE GERMAN PEOPLE..................- 67 -

INTRODUCTION

The voyage of the submarine merchantman "Deutschland" has, for a long time past, been the subject of eager speculation among the nations of the Old and New worlds.

The wildest rumours regarding the fate of our cruise have appeared in the newspapers, to say nothing of the pretty imaginative stories in which the English have announced again and again that we were stranded or sunk, or, still worse, dispatched to America in bales of cargo.

How often we chuckled on board when our wireless operator picked up one of these nice English wild goose stories from the air!

It is with all the greater pleasure, therefore, that I am now about to start on this account of our fairy-like cruise and adventures. Not that it was such a "fairy-like" business after all. It could hardly be that, for we went as far out of the way of adventure as possible.

Readers must not therefore expect to find in this little book a series of thrilling experiences such as are to be met with in the published narratives of the voyages of battleships. Our task was to bring our valuable cargo to America as smoothly and with as few incidents as possible; to get the better of the English blockade, and to return safely with an equally valuable cargo. This we succeeded in doing, as the following account will show. But as events will prove, things did not by any means always work as smoothly as they might have done, and if at times we were in a pretty tight corner and much occurred that was not on our programme, my readers must thank the amiable activities of the English for all these exciting little incidents.

In spite of such things, however, our enemies were not able to hinder our voyage, though they certainly helped very materially in making it more varied and interesting, and it would be ingratitude on our part not to acknowledge this.

And here I must specially thank my two officers of the watch, Krapohl and Eyring, whose notes have helped to make this account complete. It is impossible for a commander to be always on the conning-tower—I had almost said the "bridge" from force of habit—and six eyes see further than two. For it must be remembered that careful observation is necessary, above everything, on a submarine.

Indeed, a great number of the incidents related here came to my knowledge through the observations of my officers. Throughout the cruise they proved true and unflagging companions, and to-day they have also become fellow-workers with me in writing this account of the voyage.

My thanks are due to them, even more than to the English, and I trust my readers' gratitude will likewise be extended to them when they have read this book.

THE AUTHOR.

CHAPTER I
HOW WE CAME TO JOIN THE "DEUTSCHLAND" AND WHAT I THOUGHT OF HER

How did we come to join the "Deutschland"?

That is a long story which I shall leave the authorities to relate. The most important part of it, however, will be found related at the end of this book in the account given of our reception at the Bremen Town Hall after the return of the "Deutschland" from the United States.

To me, the idea of a submarine merchantman that has been built for long voyages is the tangible expression of the will of the German people to frustrate the effects of the English blockade of the coasts of Germany and America, and of the entire cutting off of our lawful commercial imports.

The Hanseatic enterprise, the technical ingenuity of German shipbuilding and the workmanlike activities of one of our greatest dockyards, have united in giving English domination on the sea the biggest blow it has ever had since the Union Jack fluttered over the waves.

At the same time we must not to-day overlook the changes and developments that are bound to follow in the construction and use of submarine merchantmen. Thus it is possible that the methods of sea warfare will be entirely revolutionised, that new conceptions and conditions of international law will be created, and that changes in the commercial relations of the world will follow which may influence the lives of peoples even more strongly than the present world-war is doing.

We may be proud of the fact that it is a German boat that has ushered in this new epoch.

Our achievement is not to be minimised by the fact that Canadian warships have crossed the Atlantic before us during this war. For they travelled in company, always changing, and accompanied by torpedo-boats, cruisers and auxiliaries. They contained only provisions and ammunition, and except for their armament had no dead weight to carry. But their greatest advantage was that they could defend themselves if necessary, whereas the only defence of the submarine merchant-trader lies in submerging. And that is not everywhere possible with a huge, heavy ship of nearly 2000 tons.

Well, I found myself faced with the problem of taking the "Deutschland" to America—an entirely novel and wonderful task. It would have been a new one to me, moreover, if I had not been as I was, an old North German Lloyd captain of a large clumsy steamboat, but a young U-Boat commander.

But to explain this I must first relate how I came across the "Deutschland." Events moved with surprising rapidity in connection with it. In the middle of October, 1915, I was in Berlin on business. I had then been obliged to leave my bonny steamer "Schleswig" for some time, but the North German Lloyd Company were well acquainted with my whereabouts.

One evening, whilst I was at my hotel, I received a communication, with an urgent invitation to visit Herr Lohmann in Bremen at the Hotel Adlon at the earliest possible moment.

I was surprised. I knew the name of the head of the famous Bremen firm very well, and had been personally acquainted at one time with Herr Lohmann in Sydney, where his firm had been agents for the North German Lloyd Company.

But what did Herr Lohmann want of me, now in these days of war when the "German merchant fleet had been swept from off the seas," as one read daily in the English newspapers? At that time it would have been exceedingly difficult to undertake the management of a German line to the Straits and Australia! And in the Baltic Sea the firm had no trade connections.

What, then, did they want with an old East Asia, America, and Mediterranean captain? Thus I ruminated as I made my way to the Hotel Adlon.

Herr Lohmann received me cordially and did not hold me long in suspense. He alluded to the fine old days in Sydney, asked me how I liked hanging about on dry land, and if I would care again to undertake a long voyage.

What could an old merchant captain say to this, a man who had been practically obliged to leave his ship in an enemy country, and lie about like a wreck on land, while on the other side of the Channel and off the Shetlands the cursed English cruisers lay in wait, and four miles from New York even the American post on neutral ships was overhauled?

I shrugged my shoulders and was silent.

Then it all came out.

Herr Lohmann told me straight away that he was thinking of starting a line of submarine traders to America, and asked me if I would be willing to take command of the first boat. He explained that the first voyage was to be to Newport-News, and asked me, as I had a knowledge through my voyages on the Baltimore line of the North German Lloyd ships, of the waters and depth conditions outside Chesapeake Bay, whether I thought I should be equal to taking such a submarine trader safely across the Atlantic, if the matter really came off.

It was a great plan.

I was never one for weighing pros and cons, and so I said "Yes" straight away. This was indeed a chance for a fellow of over forty-five years, in this war of "black lists" and daily postal robberies, to do something!

"Herr Lohmann," I said, "if the matter really comes off, you can count on me."

And the matter really did "come off."

Barely two months had elapsed when a telegram called me to Bremen for an important discussion. There I saw designs, sketches, and constructional drawings enough to make me open my eyes wide. And when, four months later, during which time I had been by no means idle, I travelled to Kiel, there rose before my eyes on the slips a strange steel object. Trim, comfortable-looking, and quite harmless she lay there, but nevertheless, hidden in its interior, was the realisation of all those detailed, overwhelmingly complicated figures and plans.

I cannot say that the completed reality even then helped to make more intelligible those blue papers with their endless network of strokes and lines, which had so dismayed and bewildered the mind and eye.

Any of my readers who have ever seen in illustrated papers sketches of the control-room or of the conning-tower of a U-Boat will understand this. Indeed, when they are face to face with such a wild medley of rudders, valves, screws, cocks, tubes and pipes, with such a bewildering conglomeration of levers and apparatus, each of which has a highly important meaning and purpose, let them take comfort. My impressions were just the same.

But when this tube-like monster was christened, and her giant grey-green body slipped majestically and silently into the water, she was suddenly transformed into a seafaring vessel, a vessel that swam in her rightful element, as if she had always done so. The first time I trod her narrow deck and climbed into the conning-tower and on to the navigation platform, it was only from her sides, where the green body swelled massively out of the water, that it was possible even faintly to realise how enormous her hull must be.

With proud delight my eyes travelled over the whole structure, as it swayed lightly beneath me, delicacy and strength symbolically blended.

Now I knew that what had hitherto appeared to me as a monstrous product of technical imagination, was a ship, in which I could travel the seas—a real ship—on which an old seaman could set his affections.

Then I laid my hand on the parapet of the conning tower of the "Deutschland" and swore to be true to her.

And in this manner I struck the "Deutschland" and became commander of the first submarine merchant-trader.

CHAPTER II
THE TRIAL AND DEPARTURE

And now a strange and wonderful time followed. Day after day, out into the bays, down into the depths. We practised in all weathers and under all conditions.

Every man of the chosen crew realised the task that lay before us. It meant acquiring the art of managing this most delicate and complicated vessel, the last word in bold and skilful construction. It meant learning to know and understand that marvellous wonder-work of modern shipbuilding—a submarine. We had to be in a position to sway, according to our will, this heavy mass of nearly 2000 tons, so that she should obey the least pressure of the rudder, so that she should twist and manœuvre like a torpedo-boat, so that she should rise and sink in the water like a dirigible in the air.

It meant probing the trustworthiness of the unyielding steel body, the weight and pliability of her mighty machinery; getting on the track of her imperfections or tricks, and coaxing from her the secrets of her mobility and fantastic fish nature.

A submarine is as full of humours as a woman, and as tricky as a racehorse. She is as sober as a tramp-steamer, and as trustworthy as a tug. She has good qualities and—not good. She can be pliant as a racing yacht and as pig-headed as a mule. And she only obeys him who knows her down to her smallest technicalities.

In this spirit we practised for weeks, round about, above and below water. We studied our boat, and tried not only to become familiar with all her possibilities, but to penetrate into the inner mysteries of this nautical amphibian. And when we returned from the stillness of the bay to the ear-splitting noise of the riveting hammers and the restless hum of the dockyard, we would sit for hours with the constructors and exchange our experiences.

This practical testing gave rise to much stimulating groundwork for new plans and inventions.

It is difficult to express the high esteem I feel for the men of the dockyard at Kiel, or how much I owe to their co-operation. They were untiringly helpful in explaining and testing this wonderful product of their hands and brains, in all its peculiarities. On the very day of our departure the ingenious constructor of the "Deutschland," Over-Engineer Erbach, came out to our place of anchorage to make a last submerging test.

And at last the day of our departure arrived.

The "Deutschland" was loaded up. The valuable cargo lay well packed in its appointed place, the whole boat was once more overhauled and brought into careful trim.

We laid in provisions for the long journey, and at the last moment even cigars and—gramophone records were brought on board.

With these all our possible wants were securely provided for, and the "Deutschland" was ready for the voyage.

We were ready, too. The farewells from all our dear ones at home lay, God be thanked, behind us; there is always a nasty moment in connection with a cruise into the Unknown, which it is best to get over quickly.

The last to shake us by the hand were the men of the Germania dockyard.

Then the gangway is pulled up, the crew take up their stations, and I climb into the conning-tower.

The steam-tug lies beside us and takes over the hawsers. I call down to the engine-room, "Look out!" and raise my hand. The great moment has arrived.

"Cast off the aft hawsers!"

"They're off."

"Tow away, 'Charlotte'!" [1]

The engine telegraph on the stout little steam-tug sounds: the sturdy craft strains at the tow-ropes, and slowly the stern of our "Deutschland" is drawn away from her resting-place in the dock.

"Cast off the bow hawsers!"

"They are off."

And with a smack the last hawsers fall from the pier wall into the black, seething waters of the harbour.

Now we are off. I take up the speaking-tube to the control-room:

"Port engines half-speed astern!"

"Starboard engines slowly forward!"

"Rudder twenty starboard!"

"Rudder lies twenty starboard."

Thus the replies from the engine-room come back promptly.

On the conning-tower where I stand next to the helmsman, in front of his little hand-wheel, one hardly feels the movement of the engines.

Only from the churned-up water that seethes foaming and dirty against the rounded body of the "Deutschland," quickly dispersed to starboard, is it possible to realise that the engines are working.

Slowly the big green whale's back twists and turns, lies first broadside on in the fairway, then slightly to port, then turns with the help of the tug once more to port and astern.

"Stop both engines!"

Slowly the boat moves slightly backwards, pulling at the tow-ropes in its backward movements like some primeval monster. A quick glance from the conning-tower over the trail of water and the pier walls. We have enough room to manœuvre. The hawsers are cast off, and then both engines are set at half-speed with rudder to port. We turn once more to get well clear of the dock walls where a big grey battle cruiser is being finally equipped. Then I let the rudder lie amidships and order both engines "full steam ahead."

The stern begins to tremble in rhythmical vibration under the increased engine-power, the churned-up water rushes foaming from her sides—the journey begins. Faster and faster the "Deutschland" pushes her way through the dirty waters of the harbour, out into the bay. Our course lies next through the Kaiser Wilhelm Canal to the Weser, where the shipment of the cargo will be completed.

The ship's papers and express post are brought on board by the freighting officials in a special tug, and without any fuss, calmly and secretly the "Deutschland" starts on her remarkable voyage—the first submarine of the world, to whom blockades are unknown—out into the open sea, into the freedom of the ocean.

CHAPTER III
THE FIRST DAY AT SEA

The North Sea rolls in long swells against us. The weather is clear and the wind blows sharply from N.N.W.

I am standing alone with my first officer on duty on the conning-tower, in the "bath-tub," for thus we have nicknamed the strong shelter which is built round the conning-tower hatch of the "Deutschland," and which looks like a kind of flying gondola. In front of this is the upper steering station, which can, however, only be made use of in fine weather.

To-day we stand in oilskins behind the shelter, for the sea is already quite rough enough to wet everything through. The deck is continually swamped, and every minute the waves break over the tower.

I listen with the speaking-tube to the control-room in my hand, while the helmsman growls commands through the telegraph to the engine-room. A dull roar, the bow dips down, foaming, and the waves rush over the deck and dash high against the conning-tower. As quick as lightning we close the hatches and duck in our crackling oilskins behind the shelter ... this little game is repeated every five minutes.

Between whiles we stand up, listening to the wind rattling in the stays of the masts, and look around us.

For some time the German coast has faded from sight behind us in the S.E., and the accompanying torpedo-boat which travels in front of us is the last bit of the Homeland. Soon we approach the last line of German outposts; four look-out vessels pass by us in single file and signal us "Pleasant voyage."

Our faithful companion now approaches nearer; her crew give us three hearty cheers; the officers on the bridge salute; and we two lonely men on the tower return the salute. Then the little black boat ducks into the sea, makes a beautiful turn, stirring up the foaming water at her keel, grows smaller and smaller, and presently disappears, leaving a thin drifting smoke-flag behind her.

We are left to ourselves, and travel into the Unknown.

Not much time, however, is allowed for thinking. Danger now threatens us from all sides, and I have to make certain that the boat is in good trim, and that I have the engines and submerging appliances well in hand.

I give the command, "Clear everything for a submerging test!"

At once the response comes back from conning-tower and control-room, and the crew hurry to their submerging stations. The oil engines are still throbbing and hammering. Then the alarm bell is sounded and I spring into the conning-tower; the hatches are closed, and at the same time the oil engines cease working.

For a moment one is conscious of a slight pressure in the ears; we are shut up from outside and all is still, but there is no real silence; only a change of sound.

Then comes the command:

"Open the submerging valves!"

"Flood!"

What now follows is so strangely impressive that one could never forget it, once having experienced it. The submerging valves are quickly opened, and with a hiss the compressed air rushes out of the tanks. A gigantic volume of air rises, with such an unearthly snorting and blowing that the pressure in one's ears becomes almost painful. Then the noise becomes more even, and is followed by a loud humming and whistling, and all the high notes of the machinery in the engine-room join together and produce a confusion of sounds.

It is like the strains of some mad, diabolical music that, after the dull, heavy hammering of the oil engines, gives a momentary impression of unearthliness that is at once penetrating and impressive.

This noise in the valves is a sign that the submerging mechanism is at work.

The music continues, but in a long downward scale, and during these long drawn out, ever-deepening sounds, one has a bodily feeling as of the rushing in and flooding of mighty masses of water. One seems oneself to grow heavier and to sink with the boat.

Through the window of the conning-tower and by the aid of the periscope it is now possible to observe how the front part of the boat is sinking; the railings are cutting their foaming way through the waves, while the water round the conning-tower rises higher and higher, till everything outside is wrapped in the wonderful twilight of the deep.

Only our faithful lamps are shining. Now it has indeed become silent. The only sound that reaches the ears is the soft swaying rhythm of the electric engines.

Then comes the command:

"Go down to eleven fathoms!"

"Both engines half-steam ahead!"

By the gauge I can follow the depths we are making. Through the flooding we have added several tons of dead weight to the boat. We have made the closed up ship's body heavier than the mass of water displaced—and our giant fish sinks—almost falls—into her element down below.

At the same time we are moving with the electric engines, and the forward thrust of the propeller brings pressure and reaction upon the diving rudder, and transforms the sinking into a downward gliding movement.

When the desired depth is reached, which I can tell at once from the depth gauge, further sinking is prevented by the simple means of making the boat lighter again through pumping out the superfluous water from the submersion tanks.

The furious working of the pumps is thus always the sign that we are approaching the desired depth. Then it stops, only the electric engines continue humming, and from the control-room comes the announcement:

"We are lying at eleven fathoms."

"Boat is trimmed!"

We are travelling at a depth of eleven fathoms. This means that we are practically blind and can only judge our way by the depth gauge and by the help of that carefully protected boat's treasure—the gyro-compass.

No glimmer from outside now reaches us; the periscope has long been swallowed up, and the steel safety shutters in the windows of the conning-tower are tightly closed. We are entirely transformed into the character of a fish.

Now the communications from all compartments, control-room, engine-room, stern-room, bow-room, holds, accumulator rooms, come through without a hitch. We can travel safely with our "Deutschland" in the deeps.

It is not always, however, such an easy matter to bring a boat of this size down to a prescribed depth. The changes in the specific weight of the water, owing to varying temperatures or to the different proportions of salt held in solution, play a very important rôle. How strong an influence this can prove I will show in the difference between the Baltic and North Sea waters.

The specific gravities of the two seas are in the proportions of $1 \cdot 013$ to $1 \cdot 025$. This difference in itself may not appear very considerable. With a boat, however, of the size of the "Deutschland," for the submersion of which a very heavy excess weight of many tons is necessary, very important consequences are bound to follow from this difference in specific gravity. Thus in order to submerge in the heavier waters of the North Sea it is necessary to make the boat at least seventeen tons heavier than in the Baltic, as otherwise we should not sink.

Moreover, during sudden alterations in the temperature of the water in the bays and river mouths, where the lighter fresh water comes in, the most unpleasant surprises often occur.

Many a U-Boat commander has thought it possible with a certain amount of excess weight to submerge without difficulty and to keep his boat at a fixed depth. Suddenly, however, the pressure gauge registers a greater depth and the boat drops in the water, like an aeroplane which has fallen into an air-pocket, until a test of the specific weight and temperature of the water gives the clue to her behaviour.

It will therefore be seen that such measurements are necessary before the commander can count with certainty on being able suddenly to submerge and as suddenly to reappear above the waters.

In the meantime we have finished our submerging test satisfactorily. All has gone well and each part fully performed its functions. We are in complete control of our complicated apparatus.

Now the command to reappear is given, the diving rudders are set to "up," and immediately I am able by the depth gauge to follow their working and that of our stout pumps.

After assuring myself that there is no noise of propellers to be heard anywhere in our vicinity, and that on all sides there is no likelihood of collision with any steamer, we pass through the dangerous "blind moment."

By this I mean that space of time during which the boat has risen so high that she could be rammed; while, on the other hand, she is still too deep under the water to get the periscope above the surface and take a look round.

This lasts a few minutes. I stand at the periscope and watch. Already the field of vision is lighter. Silvery air bubbles rise up glittering; a blinking and twinkling appears on the glass. Then it is day. A picture arises, clear and shining. The North Sea sways before my eyes with an empty and endless horizon.

Now we are rising to the surface. By the use of the rudder the boat pushes forward faster and faster to the surface of the water. In order to accelerate the ascent compressed air is forced into one of the submersion tanks.

Now she moves very rapidly: the tower is already free. The deck rises dripping out of the water, the conning-tower hatch is opened, fresh air streams in, and I give the command:

"Blow out ballast tanks!"

A wild howling and screeching comes in reply from the control-room, while the powerful turbine engine presses the water out from the submerging tanks.

This does not take long. As soon as a tank is empty the excess air rushes out with a pleasant sound at the side of the boat, and we are soon in normal floating trim again.

We are still using electricity. Now comes last of all the starting up of the heavy Diesel engines by the electric motors.

I have already climbed into the conning-tower and can see nothing of all this, except by the communications from the control-room. Those who are in the engine-room, however, will have an exciting spectacle.

The observation engineers stand at their posts. A command comes through the speaking-tube. Everything is ready. Then the chief engineer gives a shrill whistle, raises his hand, two quick wrenches at the switchboard in the electrical engine-room, a couple of blinding flashes half an inch long: the first valve-heads rise slowly, hesitatingly, as if unwilling, then quicker, a wild report and hissing, a wild irregular spluttering, then the loud explosions become rhythmical, and faster and faster both machines resume their regular vibrations.

The submerging test is completed, and pounding along the "Deutschland" proceeds on her way. The wind does not drop, but the weather keeps fine and the visibility is good.

No steamer comes in sight: we can remain comfortably above water. Nevertheless we need to be extremely careful in our navigation.

So the day draws to its end. But as the sun sinks, dark threatening clouds appear, prophesying bad weather for the following day.

CHAPTER IV
THE U-BOAT TRAP

And thus it turns out. The further we get from land, the rougher grows the sea. The boat is badly tossed about. I notice the roughness of the sea as I lie in my cabin, and towards two o'clock in the morning I am awakened by a "Hullo," from the speaking-tube on the wall at my head.

The watchful second officer, Eyring, announces a white light to starboard which is approaching rapidly.

I spring out, balancing myself round the corner in the control-room, over the ladders, up through the conning-tower hatch, on to the platform.

Eyring shows me at no great distance ahead a white light. It appears to be approaching. We decide not to let it come any nearer, and give the alarm to submerge. Then for the first time I realise the wonderful sense of security that the possibility of such a rapid submersion gives.

It is all quite a matter of course. Here we travel in the middle of this world-war, with an unarmed freight vessel through darkest night. A light approaches. It may be an enemy, it probably is. In a few minutes a couple of shots may flash out, several shells shatter our conning-tower, the water stream into the ship's body, and in a short while the North Sea close over us.

None of this occurs however. A brief command in the control-room, a few grips of the valves and hand wheels, and we continue our way unhurt, for brutal power may shut us from the surface of the seas, but our enemies in their impotence only cause us to lie a few fathoms deeper. We continue submerged for the sake of safety until daybreak. Towards four o'clock we rise to the surface. It is already broad daylight, but unfortunately also there is a very troubled sea. In the distance we see a couple of fishing-boats laboriously going about their business. We keep them at first sharply under inspection, but quickly discover their harmless character and continue our way over the water.

This process has long ceased to be of a pleasant character. The movements of the boat are such that existence down below in the closed-up compartments, aired only by the ventilator machines, is causing headache and sickness among the men; part of the crew are losing their appetites. Yet it is quite out of the question to remain on deck, which is continuously swept by the seas.

It is somewhat drier on the conning-tower behind the shelter of the "bath-tank" and on the lee side of the tower, which is sheltered from the sea and wind.

Here a few of the watch off duty are huddled together, holding fast to the rails, inhaling the fresh air and shaking themselves when a particularly heavy breaker rolls up round the conning-tower covering them in salt spray.

Thus we travel on the whole day.

A couple of steamers, whose smoke-clouds appear in the distance, we avoid above water by altering our course, after we have made out their route by careful sounding and observation.

This sounds more difficult than it really is. You first of all make sure of the position of your own ship by soundings and calculations, after you have roughly estimated the position of the unknown vessel on the map. If the relative positions of these two are compared on the map with the most important steamer routes, it is possible to judge with some certainty the course the unknown ship must take.

Such a calculation was soon to prove of great importance to us, and was in this case, as will be seen, of great significance.

Towards evening it clears up slightly, and the sea grows calmer. The sun sets under brilliantly illuminated clouds in the west.

All the watch off duty have come on deck to get some fresh air and smoke a hasty cigar or cigarette. Below deck smoking is strictly forbidden. The men are all huddled together on the sheltered side of the conning-tower, tightly packed and pressed against the wall.

It is a strange sight, rather like a swarm of bees, this cluster of men in rough, heavy sea clothes. There is not much etiquette observed here; I know the men have no easy job down below there, and when one of them sticks his head through the tower hatch to draw a few puffs at his pipe, I gladly grant him the short respite.

Moreover, all eyes are fixed unconsciously on the horizon, and this is a good thing. The more men there are to watch, the more can be observed, and many of our crew have the eyes of an eagle.

Suddenly in the clear twilight of the June evening two masts appear in the distance on the port side; a funnel follows, and soon the hull of a steamer appears on the verge of the horizon.

With the help of our excellent prismatic glasses we hold her steadily under observation, our object being to make out her course in order to steer clear of her.

We have soon measured her distance, and I take up the map, compare, reckon, look at the vessel again, then pause bewildered.

From the course she is following the steamer will never reach a port.

Is it possible then?

I call up Krapohl and point out to him my calculations. We have another good look through the glasses, compare maps; they agree.

The fellow is following no route whatever.

In the meanwhile we had approached near enough to make the steamer out distinctly. The twilight of the June evening is so clear and bright that we can observe her with the greatest accuracy. She is a fine steamer of medium size, and carries a neutral flag, while her hull is painted in the colours of her country.

In the middle of the hull is a long double name which we cannot, however, read.

Suddenly Krapohl cries:

"Good heavens! how is it that she is flying her flag so long after sunset? Is it mere chance, I wonder? And what does that extraordinary coat of paint on her hull signify? She is a suspicious looking craft."

I am forced to agree with him.

The apparently aimless course of the steamer fills me with amazement. It is not usual to take a sea-trip on the North Sea for amusement in the middle of this world-war!

We consider what is to be done. As yet the steamer has not sighted us; she continues her mysterious course, and by this time lies a little astern of us.

I decide nevertheless not to submerge, as our courses must soon diverge.

Suddenly the steamer makes a rapid turn and comes straight towards us. Now we can see that the sturdy neutral has swung out her boats; obviously with intent to make more complete her character of a peaceful merchantman, is ready and prepared to follow all commands.

This remarkable civility on her part is quite sufficient for us. I send all the crew below deck and give the alarm at once.

We make ready to submerge, and in doing so move towards the steamer in order to lie broadside on to the sea, which makes diving easier.

Then, to our great amazement, the following incident occurs. Hardly has the "neutral" ship observed our movements and noticed that we are submerging, than she twists round with a jerk.

As we submerge we can still watch her as she wends her characteristic zigzag course, puffing out thick clouds of smoke behind her.

This confession of a bad conscience struck us profoundly. Never have we laughed so heartily as over the flight of this honest merchantman with her unknown course.

The artful dodger thought she was found out, and feared any moment we might send a torpedo into her ribs.

And how furious she must have been! It would have been so fine to approach quite near to the "pest" in the character of neutral ship, and then at a safe distance to let the mask of "harmlessness" drop, and shoot through the portholes.

The trap was so beautifully laid. The German "pirate" had only to go just a little nearer. Instead we described a curve under water, and only rose to the surface again two hours later.

First I searched the horizon with the aid of the periscope. Then I opened the hatch of the conning-tower, which was still half submerged, in order to get a look round with the glasses. The air was clear. In the south the moon had risen, making the dusky light of the summer night even more transparent. But as far as the eye could see the sea was empty, no steamer was in sight.

The "Deutschland" could continue her way unlighted, and besides our huge delight over the disappointment of the crafty trap-layer, I had now the certainty that we could see all vessels before they could see us.

And that was no small matter.

CHAPTER V
A SOMERSAULT IN THE NORTH SEA

That night, during the darkest hours between eleven and one o'clock, I had decided to travel submerged with the electric engines.

When we submerged in the twilight of the long summer night there had been very little wind, but there was a heavy swell—a sure sign that the wind would rise to a storm within a few hours. Towards two o'clock I gave the order to rise to the surface, and soon noticed from the increasingly wild movements of the boat that the storm had arisen, and that a rougher sea must have set in with it.

At times we made regular springs, but continued steadily blowing out from our tanks and came to the surface in good order.

From the lower end of the periscope I tried to get my bearings. It was, however, almost impossible to see anything, as the periscope was continually enveloped by the heavy breakers, the dim light causing the huge waves to assume monstrous and uncanny proportions.

Now we had risen entirely to the surface, and I climbed into the conning-tower to get a proper outlook over the wildly dancing sea. It had become pleasant weather indeed! In the pale dim light was visible a seething witch's cauldron of tossing, mountainous waves crowned with foam, from which the wind tore away the spray and hurtled it through the air. The boat struggled heavily against it and made little headway. The entire deck was, of course, flooded, and every moment the sea dashed up over the conning-tower and fell over me in showers of spray. I clung on to the parapet of the "bath-tank" and scanned the horizon—a strange outlook, one continually shifting scene of mountainous rollers.

I was just about to give the order to start the oil engines working when—what is that over there?

That dark streak yonder—surely it is a line of smoke?...

Then the back of a wave blots it out for a moment from the pale grey sky....

I wait, staring through the glass till my eyes ache....

There it is again, a dark line of smoke ... and there, there: a masthead, thin as a needle, yet I can see it through my glasses; and now ... my eyes are boring their way through the glasses ... that black thing over there just visible in the valley of the waves ... the smoke above it, four low funnels....

Good heavens! it is a destroyer!...

With one bound I spring into the conning-tower, close the hatch:

"Alarm!"

"Submerge quickly!"...

"Flood the tanks!"

"Diving rudder; eleven fathoms down."

The commands follow each other in rapid succession. But to carry them out is a different matter!

To submerge head on to this sea will be from all experience sheer madness....

But what am I to do?

The destroyer may have seen us already....

Down we must go, and as quickly as possible.

Below me, in the control-room, the crew are working in speechless haste. The emergency air valves are opened, the compressed air hisses out of the tanks—the submersion valves sing in all their scales....

I stand with compressed lips, looking through the tower window over the tossing sea around me, waiting for the first sign of sinking....

But still I can see our deck, still the waves toss us up high into the air.... We have no more time to lose.

I order more play to diving rudders, and give the command, "Both engines full speed ahead!"

The whole boat trembles and sways under the increased engine power, and gives a couple of springs; she staggers and reels. Is she never going to sink?... Then with a jerk she dips suddenly under by the bow and disappears rapidly at an ever-increasing angle beneath the waves.

The daylight which is just dawning in at the conning-tower window disappears, the depth gauge shows in rapid succession one—one and a half—three—five fathoms.... But still the angle of the boat increases.

We stagger, lean backwards, slip over, losing all grip on the floor which is sinking forward ... I am still just able to hold on to the eye-piece of the periscope ... and down below in the control-room the men are holding fast on to the hand-wheels of the diving rudders....

This lasts for several terrible moments.

We are still wondering what on earth has happened, when suddenly there comes a heavy blow; we are thrown to the ground in all directions, and everything that is not nailed securely down is hurled around us.

We find ourselves in the strangest positions, look at each other, and for a moment a deadly silence prevails. Then the first officer, Krapohl, observes dryly: "Well, we've got there, anyway."

This broke the horrible tension.

We had all grown pretty pale, and now we began to try and face the situation.

What had happened?

Why this unnatural angle of the boat? And why were the engines pounding so madly above us that the whole boat quivered and shook?

Before any of us had time to think, however, our little Klees, the steering engineer, had sprung from his cowering position, and quick as lightning had pulled the telegraph round to "Stop."

As suddenly a deep silence followed.

Slowly we collected our various limbs together and considered: what had happened?

The boat was standing on her head, so to speak, with her fore-part sloping downwards at an angle of thirty-six; her bow must be touching ground while the stern was obediently oscillating in the air above water; the gauge meanwhile showed a depth of about eight fathoms.

I took a rapid stock of our situation; it was far from pleasant.

According to the map there should be here a depth of about seventeen and a half fathoms; judging from the almost upright position of our long boat our stern must be projecting a considerable way above water, making thereby an admirable target for enemy destroyers. As long as the engines continued working it followed that as the waves passed over us the propeller lashing partly in the air was increasing our power of attraction by causing fountains of leaping water and foaming whirlpools.

This Klees had realised through the mad pounding of the engines, and by his presence of mind had removed the greatest danger.

All the same we had marked our resting-place with the strangest of buoys, and expected every moment to hear bombs crashing through the stem of our boat as it hung high in the air above us....

Moments of extreme tension followed....

But all was still. The screws could no longer betray us, and it was probably still too dark above for them to be noticeable. The destroyer, moreover, had no doubt enough to do in looking after herself in this rough sea.

It will be understood, however, that we were particularly anxious to get out of this absurd position as quickly as possible.

As the boat was still quite intact and had sustained the fearful shock without the least damage, the rest of the programme was easy enough to carry out.

The stern tanks which were not quite freed of air were quickly flooded, and so gradually the boat attained a slightly more normal position. Nevertheless, she still lay far from the horizontal. She had stuck her nose too fast in the mud for that!

By this time, however, we were at least entirely under water, and could finish the rest of our work in peace. Part of the water was forced out from the fore ballast tanks, and for the rest we continued trimming the boat with the tanks until the bow became loosened from the ground. Now we began to rise, and were immediately obliged to check her in order to counteract the immediate pendulum-like tendency of the over-weighted stern to descend.

After some time, however, the balance was readjusted and the "Deutschland" was firmly in hand again.

And now we had to consider what could have been the cause of this sudden blunder on the part of our otherwise gallant boat.

A great many circumstances must have combined to produce it. Apart from the fact that it is only possible in rare cases to submerge a heavy boat in a rough sea, it is conceivable that owing to the haste enforced on us by the destroyer the tanks had not been quite pumped out.

The chief reason, however, appeared to be the sudden dynamic working of the diving rudders; this, in combination with full engine power and the downward pressure of a particularly heavy sea, forced the fateful gradient too suddenly. We found ourselves in the position of a dirigible which steers too low before landing, and through a sudden downward current of air is flattened and crushed to the ground by the double weight.

Fortunately for us, the wonderful material of our steel body stood the heavy blow undamaged. Only the bottom of the North Sea may have suffered a little indentation at Latitude X° N. and Longitude Y° E.

One thing more strikes me as worth mentioning in connection with this event.

When I look back in retrospect on my thoughts as we dived at full speed through the deeps at an angle of 36 degrees, I must confess my first thought was for the cargo! Was the cargo safely stored? Could it possibly shoot overboard?

The thought came quite instinctively, strange though it seemed to me afterwards.

I could not shake myself free of the old Adam as captain of a heavy steamer, even on board a U-Boat.

CHAPTER VI
OUT INTO THE OPEN

We had had more than enough of the North Sea by this time, and were now quite ready to get out into the open.

We were quite clear as to our route, thank goodness. Less so as to what might happen to us on the voyage; but we were prepared by now for any little surprises that might occur. For why travel in a submarine if there are no difficulties to be overcome? After all, many U-Boats had passed successfully through the North Sea and reached the open ocean. Moreover, they had had many dangerous duties to carry out, while we had only to take care not to be seen, and to slip out as quietly as possible.

As a matter of fact, it was not only that we had not to be seen. Our chief care was that we should not be recognised as a U-Boat trader.

The peculiar character of the "Deutschland" as a peaceful unarmed merchant trader would not have protected us in the least from being sunk at sight. Of that we were convinced, and how right we were was seen in the later English and French official declarations.

If we were once recognised as a U-Boat trader, we should have been not only in danger every minute, but our unhampered arrival at the American port of our destination would be highly endangered. We should have had a whole pack of thirsty bloodhounds in our wake. We hoped therefore to take the whole world by surprise by our arrival in America, and all our ambitions were strained towards this achievement.

Thus I meditated as we neared the danger zone.

We moved forward therefore with great caution. We saw a great deal in the process, were seen ourselves extremely seldom; recognised never. During the day we avoided several steamers by altering our course. At night we travelled with darkened lights, submerging when necessary.

The weather also favoured us. Once we sighted an English auxiliary cruiser some distance off; she was travelling in a definite direction with a zigzag course. For some time we held a parallel course with her, keeping her carefully under observation. But owing to the high seas, which must have made her navigation far from pleasant, we remained unnoticed.

On another occasion a look-out vessel approached us in the evening twilight; she had seen us and hailed us with the English merchant flag to signify harmlessness and thus mislead us for an attack.

As we continued calmly on our way she moved off in vexation. The sea was probably too rough for her to seek further communication with us. We were easily able to avoid other look-out vessels, travelling at an even higher rate.

Later on it grew calm—and misty. We submerged and came to rest on the bottom. We were in no hurry, and why should we not take a little rest?

It was not what might be called exactly shallow in that spot; it was, in fact, extremely deep. All the more calm and safe a resting-place. For what else were our excellent deep-sea lead machine, and the wonderfully stout body of our "Deutschland"?

That night on the bed of the ocean at X—— was a great relaxation for us all. We were able once more to have a good wash and rest without fear of being immediately awakened by a "Hullo" from the speaking-tube.

But first of all we dined—a real, proper dinner. The two gramophones played gaily, and we clinked our glasses together, which were filled—possibly out of compliment—with French champagne.

Our faithful Stucke—steward, second cook, and servant to us all—waited on us with earnest solemnity, just as if he were still steward in the dining-room of the "Kronprinzessin Cäcilie." It was impossible to imagine that he had been a prisoner in France for nearly a year. It was as if he had always haunted the "Deutschland" at a depth of ten fathoms below the sea, where in our comfortable mess-room he was continually developing fresh arts and contrivances, and had stored away in the miniature pantry and a couple of drawers an undreamed-of amount of table linen and plate.

Next morning we go up to the surface again. The pump rattles and growls and we climb with several hundred gallons over normal weight, and with the diving rudders in perfect working order, to the surface.

At about eleven fathoms the boat begins to lose her beautiful steadiness. This is first noticeable on the gauge, afterwards by the diving rudders which are harder to manipulate and on which the boat often presses heavily. The higher we rise the more powerful these movements become, so there must be a pretty rough sea up above.

We rise now carefully up to periscope depth, travel thus for a while and look around. Except for a wide sweep of foaming waves nothing is to be seen. The weather suits me exactly, for we can diminish our watchfulness accordingly.

I now decide to rise entirely to the surface, and fill one of the tanks with compressed air till the conning-tower is sufficiently free. The oil engines are started, and the ventilation machine makes ready to take in a fresh supply of air. Hardly have we opened the hatch of the conning-tower, however, when a rough, watery greeting flies down into the control-room. We are not quite ready apparently. Another tank is blown out and the turbo-fan set in motion till the tanks are soon quite empty.

But first another little trick of seamanship has to be brought into play.

In order to rise still higher we have to get her broadside on again, for in this wild sea the long, heavy body of the boat will not rise easily out of the water head on.

Moving slowly we turn the "Deutschland" broadside on to the sea. She rolls horribly, nearly shaking the soul out of your body. Added to this, the heavy cross-seas are sweeping continuously over the boat. But she obeys the diving rudders and slowly raises her nose out of the water. As we rise entirely to the surface the conning-tower and periscope sway alarmingly in the air.

Now comes another unpleasant moment. It is necessary to bring the boat at slow speed again on to her proper course.

Sheltering behind the thick windows of the conning-tower, on which the spray streams down incessantly, with arms and legs wedged firmly against the sides, I peer around.

From old experience of the sea, I am waiting for three particularly heavy waves to pass over, which are usually followed by a low irregular one. Now the third big wave has passed. There is a call to the helmsman in the control-room; it works. The bow bores her way slowly round, and we are back on our old course again without meeting any particularly heavy breakers.

It is still a pretty tough job all the same. The storm, if anything, increases, and our journey proceeds but slowly against the heavy sea. Added to this, part of the crew are seasick; and the short, backward pitches of the boat are horrible. But as we proceed, the long steady swell of the Atlantic Ocean becomes more marked. The short, pitching movements gradually cease and change into a majestic swaying.

In the distance we see two English cruisers returning from their nightly reconnoitre. We lie too low for them to notice us, and they disappear rapidly in the opposite direction.

Now we are free from the English outpost boats, and steer cheerfully out into the wide open spaces of the Atlantic.

CHAPTER VII
IN THE ATLANTIC

At last we were out in the open.

The Atlantic did not receive us in a very friendly manner it must be confessed.

We had grown used to a good deal in the last few days, but I was anxious to spare the nerves of the crew as much as possible, on account of the long journey that lay before us. I decided therefore to take a more southerly direction, in order to try and hit on fairer weather if possible. Unfortunately we were to be disappointed in this, as will be seen.

As I glance to-day through my notes of those first days in the Atlantic, I continually come across remarks of this kind: "Heavy Sea," "Stiff wind from the W.N.W., Strength 8," "Wind blowing up for a storm," "Heavy seas rolling over the whole boat and even over the conning-tower," "Boat travelling almost continuously under water," etc. In these few curt sentences lies the history of the hard and nerve-racking existence of twenty-nine men, shut up in the body of a steel fish, as she made her way untiringly through the wild tossing seas.

I know of no better opportunity of praising the excellently thought-out construction and the perfect seafaring qualities of our "Deutschland" than in calling to mind those stormy days in the Atlantic. The elements certainly did not help to make our journey to America an easy one. The highest possible demands were made on the body and machinery of the boat, which had to be continually at work day after day in order that we might reach our destination.

And here I cannot help thinking with gratitude of the dockyard and all the men whose work had contributed to help us complete our journey by giving this wonderful piece of sea-craft mechanism into our hands.

It is easy to wax enthusiastic over a fine ship, that delights the eye of every onlooker when in harbour by her elegance, and extracts the admiration of the expert and the uninitiated by her rapid movement in smooth waters. But the real inner worth of a ship is only to be discovered when she has completed her test on the high seas. Then, and only then, you learn her best qualities and gain that real confidence in her trustworthiness and seafaring capabilities, when the wind is blowing with a strength 10, and the sea has a roughness 8, during which you must go head on. And this not only for a couple of hours, but day after day, week after week. Only then can a ship prove what she is really worth.

This is particularly the case with a U-Boat in war time. A merchantman in peace time has very often a severe strain in holding out, but she has always the possibility of seeking a port of refuge, or of hailing assistance. At the worst, she can drift a few days and wait for smoother weather. None of this is possible with the U-Boat. To the dangers of the sea are added the dangers from the enemy, the cruellest and most pitiless of enemies. No haven of refuge beckons to her, and if she were to lie for a few minutes helpless and be discovered, her adversaries, who would have helped a damaged steamer in distress, would loosen the greedy bloodhounds at her throat.

No one is so lonely and entirely dependent on himself as a U-Boat captain. If he cannot absolutely rely on his vessel, then he is lost.

It is for this reason that we realised how much we owed to the Germania docks and to the chief engineer, Erbach, the inventor of our boat. It was his plans combined with the splendid co-operation of the submarine builders and shipping officials that had given birth to this wonderful seafaring vessel. The boat which in the winter of 1915 arose on the slips at Kiel, in so short a space of time and yet with the precision of accurate workmanship, and which Herr Erbach taught me to work and understand on that memorable test voyage early in the year, was now two months later bravely ploughing her way through the stormy seas, carrying the fame of German shipbuilding across the ocean.

The "Deutschland" had therefore been severely tested, and had come through with flying colours. For several days the weather remained the same, with hurricane gusts lashing up the water into crashing mountains of waves.

All the deck hatches were, of necessity, closed, and at times even the conning-tower hatch, which was so well sheltered by the "bath-tank," had to be closed by the watch-officer at every onrush of the waves.

It was far from pleasant in the conning-tower. But below deck, where the men were suffering badly from sea-sickness in the close atmosphere and with the incessant rolling of the boat, it was a thousand times worse. Many an experienced seaman made his first offering to Neptune on this occasion.

On the third day it grew calmer. The sea became smoother and we were able to open the hatches in order to air and dry the boat.

All the men of the off duty watch came on deck and stretched themselves out in the sun, seeking a much-needed relaxation.

Worn out and pale faced they appeared through the hatches; and hardly had they inhaled the fresh sea breeze before their beloved pipes were lighted.

As we met very few steamers on our present course, we set to work to give everything a good drying. All the wet articles that could not be dried down below were brought up into the air.

The whole deck was packed with beds, coverlets, clothes, and boots. The clothes were fastened securely to the deck rails, where they fluttered merrily in the wind, as if from a washing line. In between them the crew reposed in the strangest positions, sunning themselves like lizards. In order to increase the artificial ventilation of the rooms by means of a draught of air, wind-sails were hung up in all the hatches. With their jagged side wings they looked rather like the fins of a fish, and made the rounded green superstructure of the "Deutschland" look like the back of a fantastic monster whale. We must truly have presented a strange spectacle.

No one was near, however, to notice it. We sighted one steamer only, whose smoke appeared towards evening on the horizon, and we were easily able to steer clear of her.

The spirits of the crew were excellent, as was shown by the merry warbling of the gramophone from the men's room.

In our mess-room, likewise, we enlivened the time with classical music, without which life on a U-Boat would not bear thinking of. Moreover, the monotonous part of our journey was now to begin. The fine weather continued, and we met with few encounters.

I find in my journal only the following notes: "The dull period of our journey is commencing. The boat is making her way, rolling slightly, but bearing herself bravely. Now and then we go out of our way to avoid a steamer. For several days there is nothing to be seen; the gramophones play gaily, and everyone is in the best of humours. On the open sea we are entirely dependent on the weather for our comfort."

It was, as a matter of fact, the first moment that we had been able to breathe freely. Looking round on all sides one became almost incorporated with the everlasting sameness of the sea.

One day I was standing on the fore-deck. Near me Humke, our giant boatswain, squatted in the wooden scaffolding of the small central upper-deck under which we had snugly stored our lifeboat. Several lashings had been loosened during the stormy weather, and had to be repaired.

I had stood there for some time, gazing westward, my thoughts fixed on America, our destination.

Suddenly I took it into my head to broach the subject to the sturdy Humke. I asked him what he thought of our voyage to America in these days of war. What were his impressions as to the object of our enterprise?

The rascal grinned broadly and replied:

"Why, to earn money, of course."

This reply was a little too summary for my taste, and I proceeded to explain to him the real significance of renewing our commercial relations with America in war time, in defiance of the English blockade. I then proceeded to make clear to him exactly what the blockade meant.

He grasped the idea quickly, and said:

"Well, now I understand what the English are after."

I went further, and explained to him as fully as I could the meaning and exigencies of an effective blockade, and was surprised at the directness of his answer, which expressed so naively and with such confidence the feelings of the people in the simple language of our sea-folk.

"Well, they won't get *us*, any'ow! And so there ain't no sense in the English blockade, as I can see!"

In the meantime several of the watch off duty had strolled up and gathered around to listen. There they stood, broad-legged, on the narrow deck of our little submarine in the middle of the Atlantic, a handful of sturdy, unabashed German seamen.

"Men," I said, "you have heard now the reason of our voyage, but I will tell you something more. My good fellows, you have no idea what our cruise really signifies. Our gallant 'Deutschland' is much more than a mere U-Boat merchant-trader. By her means we are bringing German goods to America; goods which the commercial jealousy and trickiness of the English have so far prevented from reaching that country. And this not only to injure Germany's exports, but in order to continue their gloomy fishing over yonder they do their utmost to harm American industry and commerce.

"That is all a thing of the past. We are seeing to that. But this is not all. The appearance of the first U-Boat trader is of far deeper significance. Without even a gun or torpedo on board, the 'Deutschland' is revolutionising the entire methods of navigation, overseas trade and international rights, a revolution whose effects can hardly be fully realised as yet.

"How, in these days of warfare, have our armed U-Boats fared? We wanted to use them as a means to prevent this barbaric starvation blockade, which violates every right of humanity, and what did the English do? They armed their merchantmen and shot down every U-Boat that approached them with the object of sinking their contraband.

"That is what they call 'defending themselves.' And what is the result? We proceed to defend our skin and our U-Boats,—knowing that in every fishing vessel a 'Baralong' murderer lies in wait,—by sinking the armed English merchant ships without warning in order to save ourselves from being rammed or fired on.

"Thereupon the English shriek for help, and by reason of the existing conventions of sea warfare they win the Americans over to their side, for under the present laws of sea warfare there are no definite conditions laid down for U-Boats. We wish to maintain friendly relations with the great American people, and therefore give in. The Government which rewarded the 'Baralong' commanders has triumphed apparently, and the command goes forth: merchant ships are not to be sunk without warning.

"Then our 'Deutschland' appears on the scenes, a U-Boat and merchantman combined. Now merchantmen must not be sunk without warning, and, moreover, the present laws of sea warfare contain no definite conditions for U-Boats. A U-Boat trader, however, that must be searched before sinking would be difficult to recognise, if still capable of submerging. For then the swiftest torpedo-boat is powerless.

"The English are caught in their own trap, for the 'Deutschland' throws the whole one-sided interpretation of the rules of naval warfare on the rubbish heap. The weapon that was at first used against us must now speak in our favour.

"For the matter stands thus. If merchantmen—which can at the same time be U-Boats—may not be sunk without warning, then according to the laws and formalities of sea warfare the 'Deutschland' has rendered the English blockade futile. For I should like to see the German U-Trader that would allow an English patrol vessel to approach near enough to examine her!

"Or supposing she is not searched. Then, in that case, merchant traders *can* be sunk without warning—English traders likewise. And thus the rights of warfare will be evenly balanced once more by means of a peaceful, unarmed U-Boat trader. And this, my men, is where the enormous significance of our 'Deutschland' lies."

Thereupon I concluded my speech, which was by far the longest I had ever made.

The fine weather still continued. The barometer remained steady, the air was dry and clear. We were gradually approaching the latitudes in which fine weather is the rule at that time of the year. The warmth of the sun's rays began to be felt, and our thoughts turned towards refreshment.

This was provided us by our "wave-bath," a discovery of the observation engineer, Herr Kiszling, who otherwise showed no interest in anything but his beloved engines. For these he was full of the most touching and undeviating solicitude. Often, during a heavy sea, when all the deck hatches were closed, he would suddenly appear through the conning-hatch and push hastily through into the "bath-tank," regardless of the exigencies of higher navigation in process there.

When the officer on duty looked round, annoyed at the disturbance, there was our sturdy Kiszling, in his oldest oilskins, leaning over the side of the dripping deck—filled with care for the welfare of his engines, trying to get a glimpse of the exhaust. At the same time he must see if the ignition was working properly, if the heart-beats of his engines were carrying out their functions, and if the explosions were quite regular. He was wrapped up in his beloved machinery and lived on its rhythmical music. He noticed at once the least irregularity in its working, and spared no trouble in getting to the bottom of it.

It must have been during one of these special tours of his, which were by no means without danger, over the rounded slippery side-deck, that the inspiration came to him. In brief, he opened to us the joyful possibility of the "wave-bath."

In order to understand this, it is first necessary to know the construction of the upper part of the "Deutschland." Above the cylindrical hull, on the sides of which are the submersion tanks and oil bunkers, rises the outer ship, which gives the vessel its real ship form.

In this upper part of the outer ship, the so-called "outer tanks" are placed which, when the ship is laden, are always flooded, as water and air may penetrate to their interior by numerous openings, holes and slits, in order that a rapid filling and emptying may be achieved. The "outer tanks," therefore, have no connection with the floating capacity of the boat; they are only the result of the outer construction which above water does not follow the line of the heavy hull and tanks. In spite of their relatively unimportant functions the "outer tanks" must, of course, be accessible from the upper parts of the vessel. This is made possible by large movable steel lids and by ladders on the upper surface of the deck. Standing on the so-called tank-deck, therefore, you have a slight elevation to the upper deck surface. The sea water is continually rushing into these big spaces during the voyage. You have only to climb in through the opened plate lids to enjoy an absolutely safe and delightful sea-water bath.

We did not fail to put this into practice pretty often, and found our bath delightful. There was only one drawback to the business. If, for instance, you entered the sea-water bath for the first time, soon after the boat had risen to the surface, you found yourself not in sea-water, but in an oil bath!

The bunkers, as a matter of fact, never hold quite tight, especially after a long strain of travelling, and so it often happens that as the boat rises to the surface a curious layer of oil breaks through before she reaches the top. This layer of oil is then to be found in the "bath tank," on the lids of the hatches and on deck. Inside the "outer tanks" it naturally remains on the surface of the water, for there it is not able to mix and disperse quickly. It generally remains there a day, sometimes longer, till the oily water is drained off and replaced by new water again. The unlucky man, therefore, who took a bath during this period, emerged but little refreshed and with a shiny nickel-coated skin. This metamorphosis, as can be imagined, caused great amusement among the crew.

The fine weather now was very favourable for submerging tests, which were made practically every day. Everything worked perfectly smoothly, and we felt we could safely approach the American coast and submerge within the three-mile zone.

During one of these submerging tests a wonderful and fairy-like spectacle was presented to us. I had caused the boat to be steered so that the conning-tower lay nearly two fathoms under water. Above, the sun shone brightly and filled the deeps with radiant light. The water was lit by many colours. Around us the sea was of brightest azure blue of an almost dazzling clearness, and transparent as glass. From the window of the conning-tower I could see the whole length of the boat, round which rose twinkling air bubbles, like pearls. In strange, fantastic distinctness the deck lay stretched out before me, even the furthest bow end was visible. Further ahead was a dim-coloured twilight. It seemed as if the bow of the boat was gliding silently through a wall of opal green, which opened up as she moved, and broke into a dazzling radiant-coloured transparency of light.

We were spellbound at this wonderful sight, and the strangeness of the effect was increased by the jelly-fish as they floated through the transparent blue and were caught in the wires of the deck rails, where they shimmered first rose colour, then pale yellow, changing slowly to purple.

We were not able at that slight depth to observe any fish.

The next day a little incident occurred which afforded us much amusement, though it turned out rather differently from what we had expected.

My ambition was to follow in the tracks of my comrades of the merchant service and the navy, who had disguised their ships from the enemy by painting and clever alterations in their outward structure.

During the previous fine spell of weather we had made a wonderful trap for steamers, in order to disguise our identity as a U-Boat from ships passing in the distance. We had rigged up a funnel out of some sail-cloth, which could be fixed to the periscope with several wire rings, till it rose proudly in the air.

The conning-tower was also provided with a covering of sail-cloth to make it resemble the upper middle deck of a small trading vessel.

Thus, ready for all emergencies, we travelled on in the brilliant sunshine, till at 7.30 in the evening a steamer appeared in the distance to starboard. We soon realised that she must pass quite near to us if we continued on our present course. We held aloof from her therefore and proceeded to try the effects of our disguise.

The "funnel" is fixed up on to the periscope and rises proudly erect in the wind. In order to give it a more realistic appearance we burn some cotton waste steeped in oil at its base. Then the conning-tower disappears under the rather flattering "middle deck."

But the disobliging cotton-wool only smoulders horribly and refuses to give out any smoke. Everyone stands round puffing out their cheeks, but in vain, till the wireless operator, a shrewd Berliner, fetches an air-pump, which produces a powerful glow in our imaginary boiler. A cheer greets his handiwork, and sure enough from the upper edge of the "funnel" a delicate cloud of smoke appears, only to vanish immediately into thin air!

Laughing, we decide to continue on our way smokeless, when up comes the boatswain, Humke, with a jam-pot full of tar. The air-pump is again brought into play, and at last our funnel can really be said to smoke!

The effect is certainly startling. For the steamer suddenly alters her course and bears straight down on us!

This is not exactly our intention. The masts are immediately hauled down and everything cleared for submerging; the middle deck disappears, and with a deep bow our beautiful funnel falls together in a heap.

No sooner does the steamer observe this than she is seized with wild amazement and horror. She turns round again abruptly and seeks flight, puffing out thick black clouds of smoke which we eye not without a certain feeling of envy.

Once more we raise our indefatigable funnel. The masts are lifted high, and while the steamer hastens away in wildest flight we stand and laugh till the tears come.

The situation was really humorous beyond description.

Our beautiful disguise, which was to screen us from observation, had been the very means of bringing the gallant steamer's attention to bear upon us. She obviously took us for a wreck, or some ship in distress, and approached probably with the best intentions, to find herself face to face with the devilish tricks of one of those rascally submarines.

What must the people on board have thought when they had recovered from the first effects of the shock? Undoubtedly they would pride themselves greatly on having escaped so cleverly this new piece of "piratical" cunning.

And we should have been so proud if our disguise had only worked a little better! We were not discouraged, however, but set to work to improve on our invention, with the result that two days later we steamed by an approaching vessel unrecognised under our own powerful smoke!

CHAPTER VIII
THE INFERNO

June comes gradually to an end, and with it unfortunately the fine weather. A rising swell from the S.W. and the absence of the current which we had expected to help us along indicates a storm centre in the south, diverting the course of the Gulf Stream. Thus we travel on throughout another day. Towards evening the atmosphere becomes close and heavy and the sun sinks slowly in a misty blood-red veil.

The sky grows threatening and overcast; there is brilliant sheet lightning, while the ever-increasing closeness of the atmosphere announces the near vicinity of the Gulf Stream. During the night masses of heavy thunder-clouds roll up, the wind rises on every side, and the wildness of the running seas increases, till steering becomes noticeably difficult.

Measurements record an increase in the water temperature, which finally rises up to $82\frac{1}{2}$ degrees Fahrenheit. Now we are in the Gulf Stream, whose periphery is marked in the air above by a fiery crown of heavy tropical thunder-clouds.

Vivid sea phosphorescence and strong atmospherical disturbances are also accompanying signs of the presence of the Stream. This is noticeable from our wireless apparatus, which is strongly affected by the heavy electrical conditions of the atmosphere. Hitherto it has kept us faithfully in touch with the army bulletins from the Nauen station.

The phosphorescence of the waters makes observation very difficult. One's eyes are blinded and observation made difficult by the continuous sparkling of the surface of the sea in the blackness of the night. This state of things is far from pleasant, for we are now approaching a zone where many steamer tracks cross each other, and double precautions are necessary.

Added to this, the foulness of the weather increases. Heavy seas spring up, and a storm of hail beats down on the deck. Over the foaming whipped-up waves a wind of strength 11 to 12 is blowing.

All around over the boiling sea hang heavy black balls of clouds, from which a pale yellow light darts out incessantly—regular broadsides of lightning. Then suddenly all is enveloped in blackest night again, while at times the whole boat and the surrounding water are lit up by flashes of greenish light, in which every detail shows up with startling distinctness....

The whole air is filled with tumultuous uproar, and overhead the thunder crashes continuously. We are approaching the centre of the storm. The boat is surrounded by an unearthly storm-world. It is as if the end of all things had come....

Suddenly the head-lights of a big steamer rise up behind us. In the darkness of the night we are able to avoid her without difficulty. Like a shining vision she disappears in the distance. She is a passenger steamer who, judging by her course, has come from the Mediterranean. I must confess we watched her row of lights with a feeling of envy, till rain and darkness swallowed her up from sight again.

The next day the weather reaches its worst stage. Hurricane-like gusts of wind sweep all around. The air is filled with continuous froth. The water no longer falls in drops, but in cascades—walls of water pour down, lashing our faces and hands painfully. The air is so thick that one can no longer see through it. In order to observe anything ever so faintly, a small piece of glass has to be held in front of the eyes, with the result that a little foaming torrent rolls from the pane on to your sleeves.

The boat travels with extreme difficulty in the roaring sea. She is tossed here and there by the waves till every joint creaks and groans. Sometimes she heels over so heavily that it is almost impossible to hold on with one free hand only, to the parapet of the "bath-tank."

It is an Inferno.

But this is nothing to the hell down below, particularly in the engine room.

Owing to the heavy seas all the hatches are of necessity closed; even the conning-tower hatch can only be opened occasionally. Two great ventilation machines are working unceasingly, it is true. But the fresh air that they draw from the ventilation shaft, which is carefully protected from the breakers, is immediately swallowed up by the greedy Diesel engines. These hungry, ungrateful monsters only give off heat in return, heavy overbearing heat impregnated with horrible oil vapour, which is then swept by the ventilators throughout all the other compartments. Such ventilation can no longer be of a refreshing nature.

The air in the boat on this account has become overwhelmingly laden with moisture. It is almost an impossibility to breathe, and one awaits with resignation, or desperate gaiety, the moment when one really will be forced to join the fishes. In the closed-up body of the ship every object is covered in steaming water which again evaporates in the heat, till everything is soaked through and streaming. All the drawers and cupboard doors swell and stick fast, and added to this the wet clothes from the watchers in the conning-tower are spread out over the whole boat.

It is impossible to give any idea of the state of the temperature that then reigned in the boat. In the Gulf Stream the outside temperature was 82 degrees Fahrenheit, so extraordinarily warm was the water around us. Fresh air no longer penetrated, and in the engine-room the two six-cylinder combustion engines hammered on in ceaseless rhythm.... A choking cloud of heat and oil vapour issued from the engines and spread through every part of the boat.

The temperature rose gradually in these days to 127 degrees Fahrenheit.

And in such an inferno men lived and worked. Groaning, the naked off-duty watch rolled about in their cabins. Sleep was out of the question. When one of them was just dropping off into a heavy stupor he would be awakened to fresh misery by the perspiration running in drops from his forehead into his eyes.

It was almost a relief when the eight hours' rest was over and the watchmen were called once more into the control-room or the engine-room.

Then the martyrdom recommenced. Clad only in shirt and trousers the men stood at their posts, a cloth wrapped round their foreheads to keep the perspiration out of their eyes. The blood glowed and rushed in their temples—fever was in their veins. It was only by the greatest strength of will that they were able to force their streaming bodies to perform their allotted duties, and to keep going during the four hours' watch.

But how long could this state of things be expected to last?

During these days I kept no journal, and can only find the following note: "If the temperature rises any higher the men in the engine-room will not be able to stand it any longer."

They did stand it, however,—they kept going like heroes, doing their work in spite of exhaustion, till at last the storm centre lay behind us, the weather cleared up, the sun broke through the clouds, and the dropping of the sea made it possible to open the hatches once more.

Then they climbed up out of their inferno, pale, covered with dirt and oil, and rejoiced in the sun as if they had never seen it before.

CHAPTER IX
AMERICA

While crossing the Atlantic we had avoided approaching steamers by slightly altering our course. We had even risked being noticed on one or two occasions, but during the last days of our voyage we submerged directly a cloud of smoke appeared on the horizon. On no account must we be observed when approaching the coast, as we had to reckon with the presence of enemy warships.

On the 8th July we guessed by the colour of the water that we could not be far from our goal.

In the course of the afternoon I conferred with my officers as to the navigation of Cape Henry, the southernmost of the two headlands which form the entrance to the roadstead of Hampton Road and Chesapeake Bay.

My idea was to await daybreak at about ten knots out from the American territorial waters in order to discover whether any enemy measures had been taken. If by any chance news of our voyage had leaked out, we should certainly have to reckon with such enemy influences.

Krapohl, on the other hand, was for getting in as near the coast as possible under cover of the night, and Eyring was of the same opinion.

Both plans had their fors and againsts, and eventually I decided to continue our way carefully in the twilight, and wait to see what the weather conditions would be.

No sooner was our decision made than a stiff breeze from the south-west sprang up which cleared our range of vision considerably. At the same time, however, the boat started rolling in a very disagreeable manner, in the stiff, choppy sea that had risen with the breeze. We decided, therefore, to follow the direction of the lights on Cape Henry and Cape Charles through the night.

We proceeded on our course, till not long after a pale light flashed out suddenly on the horizon, then disappeared again.

This was the glow of the flashlights on Cape Henry—the first greeting from America.

Suddenly a white light shone out in the distance to starboard, disappeared, and then flared out again. It was immediately succeeded by a white light on our port side, which, however, continued to shine steadily.

We looked at each other.

What the blazes did this mean? It looked uncommonly like darkened warships making flashlight signals to each other. In any case, it meant a devilish sharp look-out on our part.

At half-speed, submerged up to the conning-tower, every man at his station, we crept nearer, maintaining the closest observation, our glasses boring their way through the darkness.

It was not long before we discovered that the steady light proceeded from a harmless outgoing steamer, which was already hurrying away at some distance behind us. Soon after we were able to make out from the place whence the flickering light had appeared, the outlines of the sail of a three-masted schooner, which like many coast steamers was travelling without side-lights, and only showing a white light at her stern from time to time. This was what we had taken for the signalling of warships.

Much relieved, I let the engines go full speed ahead, and soon we hove in full sight of the steady flare from Cape Henry, while the quivering lights of Cape Charles grew clearer and clearer on the horizon. Now we knew that we had steered correctly. The entrance between the two headlands lay before us.

The lights were now plainly visible. With an indescribable feeling in my heart I greeted the flare from Cape Charles, which shone out in the surrounding darkness a silent but sure sign that over yonder, after our long and dangerous journey, was firm land again, that over yonder lay our goal—mighty America.

We passed now by the various light buoys of the roadstead, and the familiar ringing of the siren buoy near by, which I had heard on former voyages, assured my ears as well as my eyes that we were near terra firma.

After we had passed the bell buoy we rose fully to the surface. The lights of several passenger steamers were visible, but they did not discover us as we were travelling with darkened lights. At last we reached the territorial waters off Cape Henry.

This was on the 8th July at 11.30 p.m.

Once inside the territorial waters we started our lights and proceeded steadily on our way through the roadstead between the capes, till we made out the red and white head-lights of a pilot steamer ahead of us.

We stopped and showed the customary blue light, whereupon the pilot steamer brought her searchlight to bear upon us, and not recognising the outlines of a steamer, approached cautiously.

She held us for some time under her searchlight, whose rays played continuously over the low deck and conning-tower of the "Deutschland." The unexpected appearance of our boat seemed so to have bewildered the gallant captain, that it was some time before he called out to us through the speaking trumpet: "Where are you bound for?"

On our replying "Newport News," he asked the name of our ship. We gave the name, but it was necessary to repeat it twice before he grasped the real nature of this strange visitor. Thereupon there must have been a great sensation on board the pilot steamer.

Then a boat approached us swiftly, and the pilot climbed up the rounded hull of the "Deutschland" on to her deck and greeted us with the following hearty words:

"I'll be damned; so here she is!"

Then he shook hands heartily with us again and expressed his pleasure at being the first American to welcome the "Deutschland" to the land of liberty.

I asked him immediately if he had had any idea that we were expected. To my surprise and delight, I learnt that for the last few days a tug had been awaiting our arrival between the capes.

We started off therefore with our trusty pilot in search of her.

In the meanwhile the incoming steamers had discovered the nature of this curious new arrival, and lit us up on all sides with their searchlights.

Thus our arrival in American waters was rather in the nature of a weird nocturne.

The search for our tug-boat was, however, by no means an easy matter in the darkness. We cruised around for some time till at last, after two hours, we found her.

It was the tug "Timmins," under the command of Captain Hinsch of the North German Lloyd.

Great was his delight, for the gallant captain, whose steamer, the "Neckar," had lain at Baltimore since the beginning of the war, had been waiting nearly ten days for us between the capes. Our long delay had filled him with distress as to our possible fate.

Now, however, he was delighted to see his long-expected protégé safe and sound before his eyes. He communicated to us thereupon the order to proceed to Baltimore instead of Newport News, where everything was already prepared for our arrival.

We parted therefore from our honest pilot, and travelled on, accompanied by the "Timmins," into Chesapeake Bay, after proudly hoisting the German flag which had not fluttered over these waters since the arrival of the "Eitel Friedrich" in front of Hampton Road.

In this manner we entered the bay in the grey morning light. Our course became by degrees a triumphal procession. All the American and neutral steamers that met us greeted us with prolonged tootings from pipes and sirens. One English steamer only passed by us in poisonous silence, while our black, white and red flag fluttered proudly in the wind before her eyes.

Captain Hinsch, moreover, in his tug, took devilish care that the Englishman should not by chance run too close in by the rudder and ram us by mistake!

The gallant "Timmins" was useful to us in other ways. Our only means of responding to the greetings of the various steamers was by driving the siren by means of our precious compressed air. This would have gradually become an expensive game, and so the "Timmins" undertook to return thanks for us with her hoarse steam whistle.

The further we advanced into the bay the wilder grew the noise. We rejoiced from the depths of our hearts at these signs of sympathy with us and our cruise on the part of the Americans.

Towards four o'clock in the afternoon the "Timmins" was able to come up alongside and handed up to us—a block of ice! A couple of bottles of champagne were quickly cooled, and proudly we toasted the successful arrival of the "Deutschland" in America, our one regret in connection with this performance being that our faithful Hinsch only came in for the corks which flew on board the tug.

Only those who can realise what it means to have lived day after day in a temperature of 127½ degrees Fahrenheit will fully appreciate the joy of that first cool iced drink.

The news of our arrival must have spread with extraordinary rapidity, for to our no small surprise, hours before we reached Baltimore, boats came out to meet us with reporters and cinematograph operators on board.

Although it was growing dusk we were fairly bombarded, and we should probably have had to run the gauntlet of a still greater stream of questions and calls if the weather-god of Chesapeake Bay had not come hospitably to the rescue and ensured us a little breathing space. A heavy storm arose suddenly, and the stream of questions was quenched by a stream of rain which fell refreshingly down upon us sunburnt seafarers. Meanwhile through the fast approaching evening the "Deutschland," accompanied by the faithful "Timmins," travelled on once more silent and lonely towards her goal.

At 11 p.m. we drew in to the Baltimore quarantine station, and for the first time our anchor struck American ground.

The "U Deutschland" had arrived.

CHAPTER X
BALTIMORE

Our first glance the following morning fell on the stout little "Timmins," who had moored up alongside. There she lay, the faithful soul—and mounted guard over us.

Shortly after, at five o'clock, the doctor of the quarantine station came along. I gave him up our health certificate, which had been carefully made out for us on 13th June by Mr. William Thomas Fee, the American Consul at Bremen. The doctor then examined the boat, and after mustering the crew set us free, and ended up by giving three cheers for the "Deutschland" and her crew.

The anchor was hauled up, and we travelled under the guidance of "Timmins" towards our wharf and resting-place at Locust Point.

Never before, surely, has a boat travelled under such conditions as now fell to our lot, guarded jealously by our "Timmins" and surrounded by a crowd of boats specially hired by the various film companies. On each boat five or six men stood ready with their cameras, and tried to rouse us to suitable cinematograph poses by chaffing remarks.

"Show your face, Cap!"

"Turn your head round!"

"Wave your hand!" These and similar cries arose on every side, while the fellows pushed and shoved and shouted like madmen.

I stood in the conning-tower and looked to right and left, waved both hands, and had no need to force a laugh, for the wild movements of the film hunters were indescribably funny.

Thus in the merriest of moods we reached our resting-place at Locust Point.

Here our Captain Hinsch had spent weeks in making all ready for us. The "Deutschland" found such a safe harbour, and was so protected by booms and netting from the approach of any strange vessel, that according to all human calculations nothing could possibly happen to her.

We lay inside a wooden pier built out into the stream, under cover of a great shed, in which our destined cargo was already piled up in waiting for us. The situation lay so apart that the connection of the pier with the nearest good road must be first explained.

The whole position was shut off from the land by a big trench and a steel wire fencing. In the stream itself the "Deutschland" was protected by the pier and the North German Lloyd steamer "Neckar," which had lain at Baltimore since the beginning of the war and now served us as a place of residence, from which we could watch over our boat.

On the other side, surrounding the "Deutschland," a regular network of heavy beams stretched out, with thick nets which reached to the bottom of the water, so that it would be impossible even for a diver to get at the boat. Moreover, day and night patrol-boats guarded the spot, among them the "Timmins," which lit up the surrounding neighbourhood with her little searchlight all night long.

Many amusing incidents occurred in connection with this.

In order that the unloading and reloading of the "Deutschland" should proceed without observation, yet another high palisading had been erected round the warehouse sheds which prohibited the least view of the ship and loading place.

The only spot from which a glimpse of the wonderful boat, even at some distance, could be obtained, was from a pile-driver which was anchored in the stream, and which was immediately besieged by newspaper reporters as a place of observation. Here they nested, holding us well in sight, and keeping watch with the utmost regularity. Day and night two men sat there continuously, perched high on the slender scaffolding of the pile-driver, in sacrificial practice of their calling!

We were also at our posts. And at night, during the change of watch yonder on the pile-driver, the searchlight operator of the "Timmins" had his bit of fun by enveloping the reporters in beams of light and thus politely "lightening their darkness" and assisting them in their difficult task. As they climbed cautiously down from the scaffolding they were each singled out by a beam of light, one after the other, like spiders with a pocket lamp.

For the rest the gallant Captain Hinsch had seen to everything, from our reception and safe guidance down to the provision for our wants on board the "Neckar."

From this steamer only a favoured few were allowed a sight of the "Deutschland," and that only from the outside. A visit to the boat was strictly forbidden.

For her own sake we should have been glad and proud to show our wonderful boat to everyone. For fear, however, of the risk of an attack, which might easily arise on the German U-Boat trader if everyone had been allowed an inspection, we dared not depart from our instructions in this respect. And thus hundreds of Americans who had come great distances, even from the west, in their motorcars, were obliged, much to our regret, to depart without having achieved their object.

The cinematograph companies, however, did not go away entirely empty-handed. I granted their wish to immortalise the crew of the "Deutschland" on her first touching on American soil, and all of us were photographed in a group on deck.

My first journey through the town resembled a triumphal entry. The car was obliged to pull up continually. Everyone tried to shake me by the hand and pour out their congratulations.

During the first few days in Baltimore I became simply an obstruction to the traffic.

In this manner we proceeded slowly to the North German Lloyd agency, which was surrounded by crowds of people.

The next step was to go through the necessary Custom House formalities. I made my way therefore to the Customs House authorities, and got through the usual examination; I was received on all sides in the most hearty and friendly manner.

Then I went back to the agency and devoted all my sailor-like abilities to the Press. I stood in the office of the North German Lloyd agency behind the barrier of the booking bureau, on the other side of which a huge crowd was pressing. I was quite alone, and had to hold my own against hundreds of men and women, who each had some particular question to put, from the most insignificant personalities up to the highest region of politics.

One lady called out:

"Do tell me, Captain, what it is like in a submarine?" Another asked with deep sympathy, "I say, is it true that in Germany the babies are starving for want of milk?" While a gentleman of extremely well-fed appearance showed his interest by the question, "Say, Captain, what do you live on?"

I was also frequently asked: "What about the Emperor's message you've brought over for Mr. Wilson?" To which I could give as little information as to the question, "When do you think of leaving Baltimore again?"

To all these and a hundred other questions I was obliged to make answer. I stood there like a breakwater, the tide swirling round me, creeping higher and higher, till my conscious self was almost swallowed up, only on the following day to reappear in bits in endless Press notices all over the world.

Meanwhile my body proceeded, somewhat fatigued, to the German club, where we had been invited to celebrate our arrival at a purely German gathering, during which our thoughts flew back with pride and love to the struggling Fatherland over yonder.

The following days were in the nature of a continuous festivity for us. Only those who know American hospitality and enthusiasm can form any idea of the cordiality that greeted us on all sides.

The people went quite mad over us, and it did one's heart good to see what genuine sympathy all the Americans showed over our journey and safe arrival, and to hear how warmly they expressed their feelings on the subject.

Everywhere we went we were enthusiastically received. They shook us by the hand, sang the "Watch on the Rhine," and expressed their appreciation by eloquent ovations. Invitations rained down on officers and men, parties and feasts were held in our honour, and on one occasion, when my two officers of the watch, who were walking with a friend in some public gardens, became recognised, the concert music suddenly stopped, a searchlight was flashed on to them, and amidst general acclamation the band struck up the "Watch on the Rhine" and the American National Anthem.

While the general public of all ranks and classes thus showed their appreciation, the American Government were dealing with the official side of the question as to whether our boat was to be regarded as a merchantman pure and simple, or whether, in accordance with the urgent protests of the English and French ambassadors, she would, in her character of submarine alone, be regarded as a war vessel.

On the 12th July a Government Commission, consisting of three American marine officers, came from Washington to inspect our "Deutschland" thoroughly. As there was no sign of armament, or arrangements for bringing any such on board, we were quite ready to show them over everything.

After a three hours' inspection, during which every compartment and corner were examined, and which cost the Commission officers many a drop of perspiration during the crawling around in the glowing heat of the boat, the Commission confirmed the purely mercantile character of the "U Deutschland."

They were at no pains to conceal their admiration for the ingenious construction of the whole boat, and expressed particularly the staggering impression of bewilderment which the complicated mechanism of all the works had made upon them.

In honour of the whole crew a German festival was started by the many German-Americans of Baltimore, in aid of the Red Cross. This was celebrated in Canstätter Park, a great public park near Baltimore, with shooting galleries, sausage stalls, open stage, dancing ground, and other forms of amusement in the open air. I must say our men stood this test on land as well as they had that on the water. They acquitted themselves bravely throughout this homage and were not awkward. When dancing began they chose their partners without hesitation, and a couple of smart fellows even danced with the ladies who had got up the fête, as if they had been used to it all their lives.

On the 20th July the "Deutschland" received a visit from the German ambassador, Count Bernstorff, who had come with several gentlemen from the summer residence of the embassy to Baltimore.

We showed them over our gallant boat with pride, although an inspection in the midst of the embarkation of her cargo and in the intense heat was by no means an entirely delightful one.

On the evening of the same day, there was an official dinner given by the Mayor of Baltimore, in honour of the visit of the German embassy, preceded by a small luncheon party at the Germania Club House.

The dinner given by the mayor—a most amiable man—was of an exclusively political character, and was only attended by politicians and officials. There was a long succession of excellent courses and wines, and according to American custom, with the appearance of the endless drinks at the close of it, many speeches were made in which the arrival of the "Deutschland" in America, and its importance in connection with Baltimore and German-American friendship, were celebrated.

Then the municipal band appeared in the town gardens and played the "Watch on the Rhine" and the American hymn, while the German and American flags were crossed.

This was a pleasing symbol of friendship and understanding between the two peoples whose interests both lay in the freedom of the seas.

While all these festivities were in progress, which took up nearly all our evenings, the unloading of our boat had been completed, and the embarkation begun.

This was quite a special chapter in itself. Messrs. P. H. L. and H. G. Hilken, the representatives of the North German Lloyd at Baltimore, had done everything in their power to make this extremely delicate part of our task as easy and safe as possible for us.

They had not only acquired, on the quiet, all the goods for our return cargo, and had them taken to the sheds ready for loading—it was a jolly fine stock, too, and many who saw it wondered how on earth such a quantity of goods could ever be stored away on a U-Boat—but they had even procured the necessary and specially adapted loading and stocking personnel—gangs of lightermen and dockers.

Much of the work on the boat and wharf was undertaken by niggers, who were closely watched for the least sign of observation powers or other dangerous faculties. Moreover, the niggers were closely searched each time before they commenced work, and obliged to strip entirely, in order to secure the boat against any attack.

The unloading was completed without any further difficulties.

The embarkation, however, was a more difficult matter. For this careful calculations on the part of our expert submarine embarkation specialist, shipping engineer, Prusse, of the Germania dock, were first necessary. Every pound of the varying weights and sizes of the goods to be loaded had to be reckoned up before being stowed in the space particularly appointed for them, in order to prevent an unequal trimming of the boat.

An absolutely exact storing was necessary, inasmuch as the whole loading space was very limited, and every box and sack must be held firmly in its position. Otherwise the most unpleasant occurrences might arise, either during a storm, by sudden submersions at a steep angle, or any other incidents, which might seriously impede our navigation.

An embarkation of this kind therefore was bound to be a lengthy affair.

The whole cargo, sacks and boxes, had to be carried by hand by the niggers through the narrow hatchways. The goods had first to be weighed, piece by piece, each separately—the weighing-inspector taking notes meanwhile and calling out the number of weights, which were then carefully indexed.

This indexing was part of a specially thought-out plan, according to which the whole packing was exactly carried out, and the accuracy of this plan was then tested by a submersion and boat-trimming test, for which our mooring-place had just sufficient depth of water.

For this test the crew all took up their submerging stations, the submersion tanks were slowly opened and the boat flooded with just sufficient water to make her float, the conning-tower hatch still remaining above the surface.

In this way the hull of the boat is made to oscillate by means of the different water loads of the two trimming tanks, and from this one can judge if the balance of the boat is properly adjusted. If after this it is found necessary to alter the weights, the cargo is moved accordingly. One last submerging and trimming test must then follow, in order to make sure that the loading of the whole boat agrees in every detail.

Thus her two thousand tons are brought into perfect adjustment in the fluctuating displacement of the water.

CHAPTER XI
THE DEPARTURE FROM BALTIMORE

Above the description of our return voyage I should like to put as a motto what the London *Morning Post* of 18th July wrote regarding the attitude of the English Government towards the "Deutschland."

"The 'Deutschland,' in view of her peculiar U-Boat qualities, will be considered as a war vessel, and be treated as such.

"The warships of the Allies will therefore make every effort to discover the boat outside American territorial waters, and to sink her without warning."

Thus ran a cablegram which reached America from London on the 19th July. Thus we ourselves read it in a copy of the *Morning Post* which was sent to us at the end of July. There was at least one advantage, that we knew exactly what we had to expect.

Never has the English point of view been so displayed in all its brutality.

We had no torpedo tubes, no guns on board, not the smallest means of attack. We had not even weapons of defence which are always allowed on every English merchant ship. The most powerful of the neutral states had moreover openly recognised the "Deutschland" as a mere trading vessel, and yet we were to be sunk without warning!

We knew, therefore, what lay before us.

It was already known that eight enemy warships with patrol boats and nets were waiting in front of Chesapeake Bay in order to attack us directly we quitted American territorial waters, and to blow us up like blind fish, with mines.

Foresight was therefore urgently impelled on us, and our only course was, with true U-Boat craftiness, to slip through somehow.

We remembered, moreover, how we had already once succeeded in getting the best of the English and French efforts. Our running of the English blockade in Europe had certainly been by no means a smooth pleasure trip.

Nothing had caused us greater amusement than the news of the delightful announcement made by Captain Gaunt of the English consulate in New York when the first rumour was heard of the voyage of a U-Boat to America. His reassuring words to the English public were: "It is impossible to send a U-Boat to America. And even if the Germans did send one we should soon catch her. A big submarine leaves a track of oil and machine dirt on the surface of the waters in her wake. Our fast cruisers would be able to follow these tracks and catch the boat for a dead certainty."

Captain Gaunt is the expert on affairs of navigation at the Consulate, and ought to know.

All we had to do, therefore, was to see to it that their second "catch" was as much of a "dead certainty" as the first.

At last the 1st of August arrived. We had taken a hearty leave everywhere, completed all formalities with the authorities, and were ready for sea and for our rendezvous with the gentlemen in front of the bay.

Our departure was delayed, as we were obliged to wait for the high tide, in order to get from the Patapsco River on which Baltimore is situated, across the intervening muddy bar out into Chesapeake Bay. The water rose very slowly during the day, as a north wind was blowing and prevented the tide in the long inlet from rising up quite as far as Baltimore.

We waited excitedly for the rising of the water, and at last, at five o'clock in the afternoon, the moment arrived. The ropes were cast off, the closely packed attendant boats made way, and the "Deutschland" pushed majestically off from the pier into the fairway. The tug "Timmins" ran alongside of us like a faithful sheep-dog, snarling at the many big and small boats full of reporters and cinema people, if they approached too closely.

There was nothing to fear. The harbour police boat from Baltimore had been very kindly lent us, and the Customs boat from Maryland had received instructions to accompany us as far as the boundary line of their beat permitted.

Hundreds of people stood on the banks of the Patapsco River, waving and cheering us incessantly as we departed, and in the harbour all the tugs hooted with the full blast of their sirens and hooters, while the steamers dipped their flags and tooted. It was an indescribable uproar. We knew as we travelled on that the thoughts and blessings of countless hearts throughout mighty America accompanied us, and anxiously awaited the moment which should bring them the certainty of our lucky escape out yonder.

As soon as we got into the fairway with the engines going at full speed, our attendants gradually fell behind. Even "Timmins" had enough to do to keep up with us. We noticed with pleasure how slowly all the American boats travelled; the cheers grew weaker and weaker, the number of boats ever smaller, and at last only the Customs' cutter remained. When towards seven o'clock she also dropped off, we should have been alone with "Timmins" but for one uncanny follower who was not so easy to shake off. She was a smart grey boat with pointed nose and flat short stern, a regular first-class racing boat which, so rumour said, had an 80 horse-power and could do her 22 knots. She appeared to have been hired during the last ten days by a man who paid the round sum of 200 dollars a day—by which it may be gathered how highly he valued this chance of a bit of sport in running a race with the "Deutschland."... By 10 p.m. a fairly roughish sea had risen. The lights of the racing boat dropped more and more behind, and at grey dawn the following morning the sea was empty—the racer had turned back home.

In her place, however, a whole lot of fishing trawlers appeared ahead of us in the dim morning light, which made us fear that even here in neutral waters we might run into a regular trap.

Cheers and hand-waving from the vessels soon showed us our happy mistake; they were a party of American Press representatives who, together with a number of admirers and friends of the "Deutschland," had refused to miss the opportunity afforded by a night voyage of giving our boat a farewell greeting at a distance of some fifty miles from Baltimore.

One steamer after the other glided by, and the next morning by six o'clock we were in sufficiently free water to make our first submerging test. I wanted to get the boat and crew firmly in hand again after our prolonged stay on land—purely on account of the "dead certainty" of that "catch."

We therefore made our first trial, and everything went swimmingly. The "Timmins" stood by and Captain Hinsch told me later that it was a marvellous sight as the "Deutschland" dived in perfect silence, only to reappear again a few minutes later like a flash, her bow foaming, above the water.

The submersion worked perfectly likewise. After this, in order to see if everything was in working order, I gave the command for the boat to come to rest on the bottom at a spot which, according to the map, should have had a depth of 16½ fathoms.

Once more all is still. The daylight fades; the well-known singing and seething of the submersion valves sounds in our ears. The gauge in the conning-tower registers 11 fathoms, 13 fathoms; the power is lessened; 16½ fathoms appears, and I await the gentle impact with which the boat shall touch on the ground....

Nothing of the kind happens.

Instead of this the hand moves round on its dial to 17½, 18, 19 fathoms. I tap my finger on the glass—quite all right, the hand is just turning to 20. "What in the name of fortune's the matter?" I think to myself, and take up the map.

Yes, 16½ fathoms are marked there and we had taken exact bearings up above.... Nevertheless, we continue to sink. Twenty-two fathoms are registered on the dial plate.

This is too absurd. I call down to the control-room and receive the comforting reply that on their big depth gauge also, 22 fathoms have been registered and passed. Our gauges coincide therefore.

This, however, does not prevent the boat from sinking.

The men in the control-room look at each other....

It is a ridiculous situation, to be sinking in this confounded silence into the Unknown and not to be able to see anything but the everlasting backward jerking of that treacherous hand on the white dial....

In the conning-tower it is no different. I glance distractedly backwards and forwards from the map to the gauge.

Meanwhile the boat sinks deeper and deeper; 24 fathoms have gone by.... The hand is moving towards 27.... I am just thinking that the deeps of Chesapeake Bay must come to an end somewhere, and that we can hardly be sinking into groundlessness ... when suddenly, without the least shock, the boat comes to a halt at a depth of 27½ fathoms.

I scrambled down to the control-room and took counsel with Klees and the two officers of the watch.

It could only be that we had struck a hole which was not marked on the map. Well, this was nothing serious, after all. Whether we had to rise from 16 or 27 fathoms was quite immaterial.

I was just about to give the order to rise to the surface, when my glance fell on the gyro-compass, which with its slowly jerking black and white disc hangs usually so serenely in its case, which is lit up from the inside....

I fell back in surprise....

What on earth had come over it? The disc of the compass had gone quite mad and was turning round and round with short jerky movements....

The affair began to grow distinctly uncomfortable. Considering that our gyro-compasses are about the most reliable of any in the whole world, and as at a depth of 27 fathoms in Chesapeake Bay the earth could hardly be revolving round us, there was only one conclusion to be drawn, and that a confoundedly unpleasant one.... We must be turning round and round in our hole, for what reason the devil only knew!

I immediately gave orders for the pumps to be started, with the result that they started rattling, but with a more clanking, empty noise, so to speak, than usual.... They did not help us in the least; we remained sticking in the mud, exactly as we were before.

This was the last straw, and I must confess our confidence began to waver somewhat.

In the meantime we had sunk a little deeper according to the depth gauge, while, on the other hand, the rolling had ceased and we lay perfectly still.

Once more I gave energetic orders to rise immediately to the surface. The pumps started rattling and ran empty again. That was no good therefore.

The situation must be carefully thought out, otherwise we should be lying in the same place till morning.

After a lot of trouble the engineer, Klees, succeeded in getting the pumps into working order again.

With a deep humming sound they started pressing the water out of the tanks—they were working! As if transfixed our eyes sought the hand of the depth gauge. Hurrah! we were coming free, we were rising, the hand was pointing to 26 fathoms ... could I trust my eyes ... what the devil was that again? ... the gauge suddenly pointed to 11 fathoms ... then on again to 26 fathoms ... and back to 11 once more....

The affair was now growing critical.... We looked at each other, absolutely at the end of our resources, not knowing what was wrong with the boat or with ourselves, nor even at what depth we were ... and now even the depth gauges had gone mad!...

In order to understand what this means, it must be clearly realised that in a submerged boat nothing can be known or seen, except by means of the hands of the depth gauge. If that once ceases to fulfil its functions correctly, then you are absolutely "at sea."

The situation had therefore grown very serious. Nevertheless, an iron calm reigned in the boat. We had the consolation that in the utmost emergency we could use our compressed air, which could not fail to bring us to the surface, even if the pumps failed us.

There was, however, no need to resort to this. Klees, who had been lost in thought, suddenly gripped hold of one of the valves—a hissing noise of compressed air, the depth gauge pointed wildly to 66 fathoms then sprang back to 26 again ... then the coating of slime which had stopped up the spouts of the gauge was blown away by a little of the compressed air.

The mouths of the pumps were also cleared by means of the compressed air of all the mud and slime which had worked in during our wild circular movements; then the pumps commenced humming in their usual tones, and the "Deutschland" rose obediently to the surface.

We had been, however, one hour and a half under water.

Captain Hinsch, in the "Timmins," came alongside much relieved. He had been unable to understand the meaning of our long submersion and had grown extremely anxious.

We must apparently have got into some kind of pit, where the sand was being "ground" and where, owing to our circular movements, we dug our way gradually into the slime and mud. I then posted the "Timmins" at a distance of two miles away for an observation of a last important submersion test.

Our aim was, without advancing, to rise so that the periscope appeared above water, which was by no means an easy matter. It is naturally much easier to get up to a certain position by utilising the dynamical lift given by the diving rudders, but in doing this the periscope makes a little track of foam through the sea, which might under certain conditions prove treacherous.

We tried, therefore, to lift ourselves from a greater depth by oscillating up to a certain height and, by alternately emptying and filling the tanks at that depth, to reach a floating position in which only our periscope should appear just above the water, and that in a vertical direction.

The experiment succeeded. We were able to stretch out our periscope feelers so that the "Timmins"—who knew roughly our vicinity—did not notice us before our conning-tower appeared above the water.

I now felt certain that we were prepared for all possibilities and could risk breaking through unobserved. We continued therefore calmly on our way with "Timmins" and regulated our course so that we reached the exit between the capes just after darkness had set in.

CHAPTER XII
RUNNING THE BLOCKADE

Night had set in as we approached the danger zone. In front of us sparkled the steady fire from Cape Henry, while astern Cape Charles threw out her lights at short intervals through the darkness. With these as our bearings we went on calmly to face the decision.

Suddenly two searchlights flashed out over the water to starboard. The accursed rays passed quick as lightning over the dark waves. I counted several seconds mechanically, then the full glare of the searchlight struck us in the eye....

It was already too late to submerge, and the treacherous light held fast on to the "Deutschland."

A rapid glance passed between the two of us in the tower, our features showed up distinctly in the beautiful free illumination....

Then we saw that the rays of the searchlight, after they had made sure of us, rose twice high in the sky and suddenly disappeared. As our eyes grew accustomed to the darkness again, we discovered two black vessels to starboard which looked like fishing trawlers.

"The cursed gang!" murmured Krapohl, at my side; "now they have betrayed us!"

And he was right, unfortunately.

For over yonder on the coast a gigantic searchlight flashed high in the sky, obviously as a signal to the English cruisers waiting outside.

"Now was the moment," I thought.

"Make ready to submerge," my orders rang out.

"Ten fathoms down!"—at the same time we took a course to the south.

Half an hour later we rose to the surface again, as I wanted to take my bearings once more. Hardly had I taken a glance round, however, than we were obliged to avoid immediate danger by submerging again. For close by, barely 200 yards off, an American armoured cruiser was bearing down on us.

She also had seen the remarkable flash signals, and was coming along to watch over the proceedings in the vicinity of American territorial waters. Although, according to the newspapers, the armoured cruiser was supposed to have been ordered into Chesapeake Bay for manœuvres, I am of opinion that the American Government had ordered the ship to go out to the three-mile boundary line, in order to watch events in connection with our escape.

I am also personally strongly convinced that the excellent tone in the officers' mess and among the crews of the American marine would not have allowed the men of the armoured cruiser, in the event of any violation of the territorial water zone, to restrict themselves merely to observation, but that they would have taken an energetic part in the proceedings.

That such a violation was not by any means beyond the realms of possibility, and that it was probably only prevented on that memorable night by the sudden appearance of the American armoured cruiser, is borne out by the following circumstance. Several days before our departure an English cruiser had passed Cape Henry under cover of mist and darkness and searched the whole of Chesapeake Bay in the most shameless manner, after which, without making her identity known, she disappeared again.

In the meantime we had quickly forced our boat heavily down by the head into the deeps, and did not rise to the surface again till the noise of the American's propeller had died away in the distance.

We knew that the most dangerous moment of our whole voyage was near at hand. We took a careful view of the situation once more, and made all the necessary preparations for our "Deutschland."

Then we submerged again and went on, all our faculties strained to the uttermost, our nerves filled to overflowing with that cold excitement which inwardly, so to speak, causes one's hair to stand on end, while outwardly one is quite calm, gripped in that icily clear deliberation which only comes to those who are fully conscious that they are face to face with an unknown danger....

We knew our way. It had been already brought to our knowledge that fishermen had been bribed to lay nets in stated positions outside the three-mile boundary line—nets in which we were to be caught fast, in which, moreover, devilish mines had been interwoven.... Or perhaps the nets might be merely attached to buoys, which we should drag along behind us, and thus betray our position....

We were prepared for all contingencies, and had made everything ready to free ourselves from the nets if the worst should happen. But the worst did not happen.

It was a dark night. The lights from the two capes shone calmly, with friendly eyes on land, while a few miles farther out death lurked in every conceivable form.

But while the English ships travelled backwards and forwards, lighting up the waters with their searchlights and seeking us in every conceivable spot, they little knew that at times, close on their heels, a periscope proceeded on its leisurely way, and underneath this periscope—the "U Deutschland."

At 12 p.m. that night, after hours of indescribable tension, the command rang out: "Rise to the surface!"

We were through.

Slowly the "Deutschland" rose through the water, the tanks were blown out and the oil engines started.

At full speed we rushed on out into the open freedom of the Atlantic, while behind us in the north-west, the English, with whole bundles of searchlights, sought the waters in vain.

They must have grown somewhat irritable towards the end!

CHAPTER XIII
THE HOMEWARD JOURNEY

Never had the "Deutschland" travelled so swiftly as in those early morning hours of the 3rd August. With marvellous speed she raced on, leaving two broad streaks of foam on either side.

The engines rumbled in perfect rhythm, the combustion was working without a flaw, and the exhaust showed not the slightest cloud, so that even Herr Kiszling was thoroughly contented, and in a moment of unconscious tenderness nearly stroked the shaft of his beloved engines....

When the sun rose the coast had long disappeared from sight in the distance in a grey mist, and there was no vessel of any kind to be seen.

We remained on the surface and raced on like the very devil. How much we owed to our engines! On our arrival at Baltimore, after our long and difficult journey they had been still in perfect condition; no repairs were necessary, and we could have made the return journey immediately without their being overhauled. And yet the engines had been obliged to work under quite unknown conditions, under conditions which like that of the terrible temperature in the Gulf Stream had made the very highest and most unforeseen demands on every part of the machinery.

It can be easily understood that hitherto there had been no opportunity of testing the working capabilities of oil motors in an outside temperature of 127 degrees Fahrenheit. Such a contingency could never have been foreseen in the construction of our type of boat, and the fact that our motors never struck, that not the least hitch arose, proves the excellence of the construction and the perfect workmanship of the dockyard.

Thus we continued on our way, and only too soon found ourselves in the damp heated atmosphere and heavy air of the Gulf Stream, with all its beautiful phenomena and peculiarities, its electrically laden air and stormy sea. With closed hatches and heat in the boat we faced it once more. And the Stream would not even help to push us along on our course, as we had hoped.

All hardships were, however, borne with light hearts this time. We had left the danger zone behind us, and were homeward bound. Moreover, the sea had become calmer the nearer we approached the area of the Gulf Stream.

On the evening of the second day it had become possible to open all the deck hatches again. Hardly had we begun to rejoice that the fresh air would now make conditions below deck bearable once more, when suddenly the order came, "Close hatches!" "Submerge!"

A steamer had appeared and was rapidly approaching so directly in our course that we could not possibly have avoided her above water.

When we rose to the surface again an hour later night had set in, and with it appeared a most marvellous natural phenomenon of sea phosphorescence of unearthly splendour.

We had submerged in a calm dark sea; we now arose to an ocean of flame. A sea phosphorescence had set in of an intensity and glow such as I had never before experienced, and which is probably only to be found on the borders of the Gulf Stream.

During our rise, and when we were at about 2 fathoms below the surface, it seemed as if we were working upwards through a glowing realm of sparkling transparency. Shortly before the conning-tower arose above water I glanced round astern, and saw the entire hull of the boat, with the stern like a dark mass pushing its way through the glowing element. A fiery whirlpool radiated from the propeller, and every movement of the boat aroused the wildest phosphorescence—intensive flames, sprays of sparks, and fiery streaks in the surrounding waters.

Above, a fresh breeze had set in and whipped the seething waters into glowing balls, while showers of sparkling foam covered the entire deck. As far as the eye could reach the surface of the sea was one pale glowing mass, through which our boat ploughed its way in furrows of fire.

We stood transfixed as the phenomenon increased in intensity with the sea and wind.

All the men off duty came up and stared out at this enchanting spectacle, little heeding the seas which swept over the deck, soaking many of them through to the skin.

"It looks like fire, don't it? But blowed if it don't put yer pipe out," remarked our giant boatswain. A spurt had just extinguished his pipe for the third time, and he reluctantly decided to store the beloved stump carefully in his pocket.

But the "fire" grew wetter and wetter, and within half an hour the officers on duty and look-out stood once more alone up in the conning-tower.

When we got out of the Gulf Stream we had several days of stiff north-westerly winds and high seas, until, on the ⸺ August, we ran into fine weather again.

On one of the following evenings the first officer on duty, Krapohl, was standing with Humke in the conning-tower scanning the horizon without ceasing, through the glasses, at a point where the pale sky seemed to merge into the sea without any observable boundary line.

"Light ahead," announced Humke suddenly.

"If you mean that star, I've noticed it already," the officer replied, calmly lowering his glasses.

"Wal, I dunno, but that there ain't no star, Herr Krapohl," the sailor replied, unabashed.

The two called out to me, and I came expectantly out of the tower, took the glasses and then laughed.

"Humke, you're on the wrong track!" for I noticed high up above the horizon a faint white light which stood too high, judging by its strength, to be a ship's light.

The boatswain stolidly maintained his opinion, however.

"Cap'n, that there ain't no star."

I handed him the glasses which he, however, put aside at once, remarking:

"Ye can't see nothink properly with them things."

He shut his eyes tightly, then took another sharp look and said in decided tones:

"That ain't no star; that be a light!"

We stared before us with increased sharpness till I was able at last to make out through the glasses a red glow which now became visible to the right of the white light. Now we knew that a steamer was approaching us.

At first I held her to be a small vessel, particularly as, to begin with, the height of the two lights differed but slightly—the red port light of the steamer was not much below the white light.

But soon I was surprised to observe how noticeably the red light moved, that is to say, how quickly the space between the two lights appeared to increase.

From this there was only one possible conclusion to be drawn, and that was that the vessel was approaching with extraordinary rapidity.

While I was considering this, and picturing it to myself as a swiftly travelling destroyer, I discovered at a fair distance behind the two lights something that looked like a white moving ray, or like a faintly illuminated wave.

We could not make out what this meant till I decided that this wave must belong to the lights themselves, as they moved together and kept pace with each other. And a few minutes later there appeared tremblingly on the strong lens of the glasses the faint outline of a mighty steamer, which with elaborate superstructure was approaching in the dark night. The white ray of light was her stern water, which owing to the colossal length of the ship was only visible at a considerable distance from her side lights.

For some minutes longer we continued to stare, then we discovered four towering funnels, and were soon convinced that we had a big Cunard liner in front of us which was racing up in semi-darkness, only showing her head-lights.

It really was a ghostly apparition, to observe how the mighty darkened ship raced on through the night. There is not much need to be romantically inclined in order to picture this meeting with the "Flying Dutchman," while Humke expressed his feelings in the words: "Lor', ain't she just a beauty, lads!"

"Full speed ahead!" and with "helm hard astarboard" we slipped away from the course of the mighty Cunarder. All the men of the watch off duty meanwhile had come up to get a view of her from the deck and hatches.

In spite of a sharp look-out nothing appeared in sight during the next few days. The weather keeping fine our homeward journey—even more than when we were outward-bound—assumed the character of a peaceful, uneventful business voyage.

It was now that we first began fully to appreciate the convenient and practical inner fittings of the whole boat, and particularly our cabins and cosy little mess-room. Often as we sat round the table at mess while the gramophones played gaily, we thought with gratitude of those who had not only invented the seaworthy shape of our boat, but had fitted her interior up so that a life of comparative comfort and ease was possible even under the sea.

When on these occasions our gallant Stucke, with his blonde white hair, his honest face full of earnest gravity, and his habitually surprised expression placed a bottle of good red Californian wine in front of us, as we lay comfortably "somewhere" at the bottom of the sea, while overhead, at a height of X fathoms, a hearty wind was blowing, it needed little imagination to picture oneself as a second Captain Nemo, who with his highly modern Nautilus could probe the depths, and snap his fingers at the injustice and tyranny of a certain people—provided, that is to say, one had read Jules Verne.

For I must here confess, what I had hitherto carefully concealed from everyone, that it was only as captain of a submarine trader on my return journey from America that I was enabled to make good a very sad deficiency in my education. The chance I had wasted in my youth I now came across at the age of forty-nine in the steel body of the "U Deutschland," of making myself acquainted with Jules Verne's *Twenty Thousand Leagues under the Sea*.

The book had been sent me while I was at Baltimore through the kindness of an American friend. It is a book—how shall I describe it?—of incitement and emulation. I read it with the greatest interest.

The rest of our return journey is soon told. We travelled on smoothly and peacefully homewards, avoiding a few distant steamers above water—in which little game we had gradually become extremely well practised—and meeting on the whole with good weather, some mist, and much smooth sea.

One afternoon I was sitting working at the writing-table in my cabin, when suddenly I heard from the control-room close by the order "20 to starboard" repeated. Immediately after came "10 to port," whereupon, without waiting to hear any more, I hurried on deck.

There a strange sight awaited me. All around, as far as the eye could reach, the sea was covered with a mass of dark, floating oil casks through which we had to steer our way.

At first I took the black, weird-looking objects, which danced up and down on the waves before us, for a mine-field, until the characteristic shape of the sharp angular casks, or so-called barrels, and their contents which had spread partly over the water, testified to their harmlessness. Nevertheless we had to steer carefully through this strange plantation, as the area was too wide a one to avoid without going considerably out of our course. We estimated the number of casks that were visible to us as at least a thousand.

"Fine practice," remarked Krapohl, "for the elegance with which we shall twist through the English mine-fields later on. I think we might risk the return through the English Channel."

We went on, therefore, at half-speed to port—starboard—port, for over an hour. Scattered parts of vessels were to be seen on the water, possibly the results of wrecks or mines.

We must by this time have gradually come within the sphere of the English look-out ships. The watch was doubled, everyone standing at their submerging stations.

From time to time we noticed vessels whose attention we avoided by submerging or altering our course. One warship, apparently a small English cruiser, we allowed no possibility of seeing us by immediately diving. When, after an hour's undersea journey, we again rose slowly to the surface, we saw from a depth of 6½ fathoms, through the periscope, another English ship, and went down again to 11 fathoms, and this was repeated three times in succession.

At noon we rose at last for good, emptied the tanks, and then travelled at top speed over the water.

Favoured by the fine weather we approached our goal with considerable rapidity; and on August —— at eight o'clock in the evening, we saw a circle of white lights all round the horizon.

Our natural fear was, of course, that we were surrounded; if we turned to starboard we saw those accursed lights, to port—there they were too.

Finally our excellent Zeiss glasses removed our fears that at the last moment with the homeland already in sight we had fallen into a trap. The twilight was still clear enough to allow us to see and recognize from the construction of the uncanny-looking ships that only some harmless Dutch fishing boats lay before us.

CHAPTER XIV
THE ARRIVAL

Favourable winds astern helped us on towards home. On August —— at six o'clock in the morning, our alarm was raised once more. In the far distance something appeared on the water which looked like the sail of a boat, though certainly of a very strange appearance. As it approached nearer the sail turned out to be the conning-tower of a U-Boat, which, with her deck still dripping, was going on her way.

Although we were at first inclined to take careful and instructive observations of the strange object in the distance, in order to judge how we ourselves showed up at a distance of three knots, the best course in our case appeared to be to find out as quickly as possible if she were an English or a German submarine.

We preferred, however, in any case to make ourselves as unnoticeable as possible, and in the last emergency to submerge.

We had already flooded up to tank 3, already the sea broke over the deck and struck against the conning-tower, and even the latter was cutting half-way down through the green waters—when suddenly a well-known flag signal rose yonder, which gave us the certainty that it was a German U-Boat in front of us.

We answered immediately, and gave the command directly after:

"Empty the ballast tanks!"

Never had I given orders with such a cheerful heart on the "Deutschland" before, and never was it more cheerfully carried out than when I called down to the control-room:

"Hurrah! the first German U-Boat in sight!"

What did it matter that we were standing on the tower and the barely risen deck in oil and sea water with a shower-bath playing over us?... There, over the green North Sea, came the first greeting of Germany, the mighty Fatherland, towards us! At full speed we rushed on, everyone on deck, and before long the two boats lay within calling distance of each other.

The first ear-splitting hurrah was flung across to us, and answered in like manner.

Then greetings and news were exchanged, and our ways parted again ... ours towards home, the U-X to her work.

The day drew in and night fell once more. So we travelled homewards, no light on deck, no light in the tower—like a dark shadow.

When the sun rose, however, on the following morning, we saw before us in the distance a characteristic silhouette, breaking through the veil of mist in a rosy light. An island, a bulwark in the North Sea—Heligoland lay before us.

Soon life began to awaken on the waters around us. Torpedo-boats shot up, patrol boats hurried along, flag signals fluttered in the air, wireless signals rattled out their greetings, and shouting and hand-wavings commenced, and then the iron ring of the German Fleet, which keeps safe watch over yonder, closed round our little "Deutschland," and under their protection we steered on past Heligoland towards the home haven.

But as we approached the well-known waters, even before the low homelike sandy coast came in sight, a wonderful spectacle fell to our lot, the strangest of greetings carried out with the utmost skill.

From the land two huge birds seemed to rise into the air—two seaplanes which approached at full speed and then sank like gigantic water-fowls on the gently moving surface of the sea.

They shot down with their floats just brushing the surface of the water, till within a stone's throw of the "Deutschland," made a lightning turn, crashing by us, approached again and sprang literally over our heads, racing low down over the conning-tower, with cheers and waving of caps....

This was our reception from the latest weapon of the German Navy.

One should not make comparisons. But as we once more approached the German coast, surrounded and protected by the German Marine, I suddenly found myself comparing this with our arrival in America.

No one could have been received with more hearty enthusiasm than we had been by the Americans. A free, untroubled people, they rejoiced in a bold deed, and openly declared their sympathy for a new and unheard of enterprise, which it had required men to fulfil.

But here we were more than bold and interesting adventurers. Here our own people received us again as helpmates in their mighty struggle. Here the delightful spectacle of her power under the sea, on the sea, and in the air was presented to us.

This was for me the real meaning of the glorious greeting of our airmen. This was what I felt as the look-out boats accompanied us safely as far as the outer Weser, where we cast anchor before the Hohenweg lighthouse, for the first time after many a long day.

CHAPTER XV
THE RECEPTION OF THE "DEUTSCHLAND" BY THE GERMAN PEOPLE

From the outskirts of Heligoland as far as the outer Weser we had been received by the Navy. On the voyage up the Weser and at Bremen the whole nation received us.

On the afternoon of the 23rd August the "Deutschland" had struck anchor at the mouth of the Weser. The news had been spread by telegraph throughout the whole country—this longed-for news, which awakened unbounded rejoicings.

We learnt to our surprise and proud delight that the arrival of the "Deutschland" was to inaugurate a festive holiday for the whole German people, that such a reception awaited our little boat on the banks of the Weser as surely never fell to the lot of any "lucky ship" before. Our journey up the Weser assumed the nature of a triumphal procession. Behind the hundreds of thousands who had come to meet us and stood cheering on the banks, stood invisible the millions of German people inspired with the same feeling.

This was expressed to us everywhere in overwhelming rejoicings from old and young, high and low, from the German Kaiser down to the merest dock worker and the small ragged urchin who, full of enthusiasm, waved his flag and shouted in the streets of Bremen.

On the 25th August, early in the morning, the "Deutschland" commenced her triumphal trip up the Weser. It poured in torrents, but nothing could quench the public rejoicings as we moved along accompanied by the blockaded steamers, our masts and conning-tower decorated with garlands of roses.

Low hung the dark clouds in the heavens, and the rain pelted down on the thousands who stood on the dykes or who had come to meet us on steamers, barges, launches, and rowing boats. Deafening cheers arose from the town, and the clashing of bells mingled with the joyful acclamations, while above it all rose the song of "Deutschland, Deutschland über alles," which on that very day was celebrating its seventy-fifth birthday.

In Nordenham, Brake, Blumenthal, flags salute, guns thunder out, factory and steamer whistles send their piercing greetings; shouts of welcome and good wishes ring out from the North German Lloyd steamers, to which we respond by waving back.

Vegesack is passed, where work on the Vulcan Docks has ceased, the dockers standing in hundreds on the quay. Their wild cheers accompany the

"Deutschland" on her triumphal way. The inhabitants of Vegesack are all assembled at the landing-place and on the banks behind.

Again music and singing, the roar of guns and storms of rejoicing! Thicker and thicker grow the crowds as the ship nears her home haven.

Shortly before twelve we reached Lankenau, whose dyke had been chosen as an observation point by the whole of Bremen, it appeared. Elbow to elbow the people stood waving with hats, umbrellas, handkerchiefs, hands....

At noon punctually the "Deutschland" sailed into the open harbour, and placed her invited guests, 'mid sounds of "Deutschland über alles," on the highly decorated pontoon, on which the Grand Duke of Oldenburg, the representatives of the Bremen Senate and burghership, the civilian and military authorities, the marine, the shipping officials, etc., and among them Count Zeppelin, were all assembled to receive us.

As soon as the ship was moored I called the men up to take their positions on deck. Dr. Lohmann then addressed us in the following speech:

"Your Royal Highness, Your Magnificencies, Your Excellencies, My very honoured friends,—At this historical moment of the happy return of the first submarine merchant-trader of the world, after a voyage of 8,500 knots, I here welcome our 'Deutschland' and her gallant crew, not only in the name of our shipping officials, but of the whole German people, back to the harbour of their homeland. Quietly and only known to an initiated few, they left the Weser, passed through and under the English Fleet, to arrive on the 10th July at Baltimore with a valuable cargo of dyes. Their arrival was a surprise to the whole world. Even navigation experts shortly before this event had declared it to be an impossible undertaking.

"It is with particular pleasure that I am able to state that all true Americans who are not demoralised by a degrading Mammon service to England—men with the freedom-loving instincts of a Washington and a Franklin, greeted the arrival of the 'Deutschland' in America with warmest satisfaction. It is the pride of our shipping officials that we have been able to send dyes to America under the German flag in the middle of this war, while America herself cannot even get her post from Europe unmolested, to say nothing of the many other violations of the rights of humanity by sea and land on the part of our enemy, in connection with the neutrals, and particularly the small states.

"To accomplish this has been the work of the crew of the 'Deutschland.' Though they started off without any previous announcement, their departure from Baltimore was made publicly known beforehand. 'It resembled a triumphal procession,' wrote Havas, 'and a symbol of freedom.' I myself should like to compare the deed with our German view of the 'Rights of the

Peoples on the free Ocean.' The enemy were not able to prevent their departure from Chesapeake Bay, and a blockaded North Sea did not exist for them on their return voyage, as will be proved by the many million marks' worth of goods which have to-day been brought from America, and which lie at this moment before our eyes.

"They have performed a task of seamanship that is worthy of our Hanseatic forefathers. Everywhere throughout German lands, and among our faithful allies, but particularly among our brothers in the trenches and in the fleet, their return voyage has been followed with deepest sympathy. With strongest confidence in their judgment, energy, and sense of duty, we members of the shipping world have looked forward to their return. After their long and strenuous weeks in the narrow confines of a ship, face to face with unscrupulous enemies, I welcome them heartily back to the Homeland. In the midst of this murderous war I convey to them the thanks of our German people for their peaceful deed. And I should like to express these thanks by calling for three cheers for the 'Deutschland,' her commander, Captain König, her officers and crew. Hurrah! Hurrah! Hurrah!"

I answered with a brief toast to the Senate and burghership of the free Hansa city Bremen. We then boarded the pontoon, where each one of us was saluted and drawn into conversation by the Grand Duke of Oldenburg and the other gentlemen present.

After completing a distance of 8,450 knots, from which only about 190 under water must be deducted, the first submarine merchant-trader had reached home. The "Deutschland's" first voyage to America was completed.

On the evening of this memorable day a big dinner was given at the Town Hall by the Municipality of the borough of Bremen, to celebrate the homecoming of the "Deutschland." The speeches that were delivered on this occasion give a short outline of the circumstances which led to the building of the "Deutschland," and for this reason they shall be repeated here.

Dr. Barkhausen, the Mayor, had received his guests with words of hearty welcome, and informed them of the Municipality's decision to have a special medal struck in memory of the day, and had then toasted the German shipping officials, and the crew of the submarine merchant-trader "Deutschland."

In the name of the Shipping Federation, their chief representative, Dr. A. Lohmann, replied in the following words:

"Your Magnificencies, Your Excellencies, my most honoured gentlemen,— In the name of the commander of the 'Deutschland,' Captain König, and of his officers and crew, I wish to express to the Municipality their most heartfelt thanks, as also that of the Shipping Federation, for the great honour granted by the Municipality to the crew of the 'Deutschland' in allowing a medal to be struck in commemoration of this peaceful commercial deed in the midst of war.

"I wish to thank your Excellencies for the words in which you have graciously acknowledged the work of my colleagues and myself. Since the outbreak of war I have gladly and willingly devoted my efforts towards the welfare of the State. The conviction that our splendid people, in spite of the superior force of the enemy, are not to be crushed in this defensive war for their individuality and freedom, that the intellectual power and forethought which inspire our entire people, their thorough training since the wars of liberation, and the inborn sense of duty which has come down to every German in flesh and blood, are not to be overcome, this conviction has accompanied me throughout all my efforts, and everywhere I have met faithful colleagues who were of the same opinion.

"I should like therefore at this point to express my heartfelt thanks to all my fellow-workers, and in particular to Herr Direktor Stapelfeldts, and my colleagues on the Board, Herr General-Direktor Heineken, and Herr Hermann, Councillor of Commerce. The German Ocean Shipping Federation was formed, as your Excellencies have already stated, in all secrecy, and their task consisted in forwarding goods of the utmost possible value.

"It meant, moreover, purchasing the raw materials on the other side, their careful warehousing, the placing of the 'Deutschland' in a safe position, and protecting her from all attacks. This was carried out to perfection by the North German Lloyd agents, Herr Paul Hilken and his father, Herr Hilken, Senior, as well as by Captain Hinsch and his co-operators. The share which Captain König and his officers and crew took in the enterprise has already been brought into prominence by your Excellencies. For my part and on behalf of the shipping directors, I should like here once more to tender our fellow-workers on the 'Deutschland' our very hearty thanks.

"It will interest the gentlemen present to hear something of the history of the German Ocean Shipping Federation and of the 'Deutschland,' the 'Bremen,' and her as yet unnamed sister ships.

"When in September, 1915, it became evident that, in spite of all the successes of the Central Powers, the war would continue for many months yet, it was obvious that Germany's demand for rubber and metals was of burning necessity.

"I therefore took the shipbuilding authorities in Bremen into my confidence, after I had held counsel with one of the most prominent shipbuilding experts. The 'Weser' declared itself ready to draw up and carry out the plans for a submarine boat of about 500 tons carrying power. On the 3rd October I came into possession of the completed plans of this boat. The period of construction unfortunately ran into eleven months, the delivery being therefore completed about September 1st, 1916, for the docks were first obliged to have the motors built. It was obvious that we must make an effort another time if possible to reach our object more quickly. Almost at the same time that the practical evolution of a submarine merchantman was under our consideration, the Germania Dock at Kiel had, unknown to us, handed over at the beginning of October to their chief house, Friedrich Krupp and Sons, plans for the construction of a U-Boat of about 700 tons carrying capacity.

"The Germania Docks were prepared, in the short space of six months, to deliver the first boat, the 'Deutschland,' as early as April.

"Both plans, those of the Germania Docks as well as my own, showed that the project was possible to carry out, and I should like to compare this community of ideas with a happy marriage, where husband and wife are in perfect harmony with each other—the dockyard, as the mother who brings the child into the world and gives it to the father—the shipowners and commerce—to place it in the world. The soul and mind of the child were incorporated in our Captain, our officers and crew, who have performed the glorious task of taking the 'Deutschland' to America and back.

"On the 15th October we had come to an agreement, and the construction of two boats was taken over by the Germania Docks from the Syndicate. The formal part of the establishment of the German Ocean Shipping Federation was delayed somewhat. Its establishment took place on the 8th November, and the boats which had in the meantime been ordered by our Syndicate were already under construction as far as their framework. The 'Deutschland' was delivered over to us at the beginning of April.

"It was a wonderful masterpiece of the Germania Docks, and, as is usual with all the work of Messrs. Friedrich Krupp and Sons, it was perfectly carried out. Before we sent our 'Deutschland' to America, we made trial trips with her for over two months. The execution of the work proved to have been carried out perfectly in every respect. Captain König was able to announce from America that after a voyage of over 4,000 knots ship and machinery were in perfect working order; his report on arriving here in Bremen harbour was just the same. It is a masterpiece of German technique, and the name of Messrs. Krupp and Sons appears in shining colours once again.

"From the creation of our artillery, from the 42's down to the smallest specimen of ship guns that began successfully to break the chain of the

British Fleet in the Skagerrack and prepare the way for free trade among the nations, to the production of arms and war material of every description—the German people now owe their thanks for this perfect piece of construction to the ingenious leaders and directors of the greatest works in the world. Without Krupp, our enemies would not now, after two years of war, be standing everywhere on the other side of their boundary lines.

"The intelligent co-operation of mind and body, the employment of all the newest scientific discoveries, added to the true German sense of duty, these are the qualities that have made Krupp and Sons famous. To-day, on the return of the 'Deutschland,' we are face to face with another wonderful production of shipbuilding technique on the part of the firm of Krupp, and for this also the German people owe their thanks to them. I should like to ask you all, gentlemen, to give expression to these thanks by joining with me in three hearty cheers.

"The firm of Friedrich Krupp and Sons, Germania Docks. Hurrah! Hurrah! Hurrah!"

After the next course, Herr Zetzmann, the Director of the Germania Docks at Kiel, proceeded as follows:

"Your Magnificencies, Your Excellencies, Most honoured gentlemen,—To my lot has fallen the honour of expressing in the name of the firm of Friedrich Krupp and Sons and of the Germania Docks, our heartiest thanks for the invitation that has been extended us to-day by the Municipality, and I also take the liberty of extending my thanks to the distinguished guests of the Corporation assembled here.

"... Herr Lohmann has made some interesting communications in his speech with regard to the history of the origin of the German Ocean Shipping Federation, and I should like to add a few words about the workshop from which the 'Deutschland' and 'Bremen' sprang. We had been forced to admit for some time past, that owing to the continued duration of the war the need of certain building materials was becoming increasingly urgent.

"From the conversational remarks 'it might be possible,' and 'we really ought to,' arose the decision to consider seriously the possibility of a new kind of trading vessel.

"The decision was no easy one, not merely because we feared the difficulty of construction, but because we hardly dared to place a fresh load on our building yards, which were already heavily overburdened with war orders. But necessity teaches how to beg,—and also how to construct! We next tried to work on the foundations of our war boats, in the hope that by this means we should lessen the constructional work. We found, however, that on these lines reliable tonnage capacity and carefully measured space were not to be attained.

"Our leading constructors advised me, therefore, to go radically to work, and not to try and make a trader out of a warship, but to create a new type of trading boat altogether. The shape of this was to be made full and rounded, and exact calculations gave us a better tonnage, much to our surprise and pleasure, than we had anticipated at the commencement of our project. With wild enthusiasm our constructors completed their plans, and soon we stood face to face with a picture whose transformation into reality would express our every wish.

"... Herr Krupp von Bohlen and the Directors seized on our proposal with the greatest energy ... and declared that a boat of this type must most certainly be produced, and in the shortest possible space of time, that moreover the Germania Docks would begin directly on the construction of the boat on their own responsibility.

"... Everything went like clockwork.... There remains only one thing more for me to say. That we succeeded in completing the first boat in so short a space of time is due in a great measure to our principal firm and to our contractors, who delivered all our building materials and necessary fittings in spite of the other great demands that were made upon them, with astonishing rapidity.

"I wish particularly to express my appreciation that all the dealings with the German Ocean Shipping Federation, and later with the staff of the boat, were completed in the most friendly of spirits. Both Shipping Federation and command staff have met all our proposals with the greatest confidence.

"It is owing to this intelligent and broad-minded preference that the rapidity of the construction was made possible, and that the trial voyages went so smoothly. With the greatest confidence, therefore, we saw the ship undertake her first voyage.

"Our confidence has brilliantly justified itself. Our most ardent wishes with which we followed this product of our dockyard have been fully realised.

"We wish the Shipping Federation further brilliant successes of this kind, the 'Deutschland' and her sister ships many equally happy voyages, for the welfare of our beloved Fatherland, and for the glory of our revered Hansa city, Bremen.

"To-day's celebration will be for all who have taken part in it a remembrance that they will carry to the end of their lives, and the celebration has been brought to a close in the most approved fashion by the dinner given in the new Town Hall by the Municipality. When this new part of the Town Hall has grown as time-worn as the old, perhaps tales will be told of how the successful ocean voyage of the first submarine merchant-trader in the world was celebrated here.

"Together with our thanks for the splendid feast, I should like to join my good wishes for Bremen, and I ask the honourable gentlemen present to join in the toast: 'Long life and prosperity to the Municipal Corporation of the free Hansa City of Bremen and to the town of Bremen. Hurrah! Hurrah! Hurrah!'"

Footnotes

[1]: "Charlotte" is presumably the name of the tug.

www.ingramcontent.com/pod-product-compliance
Ingram Content Group UK Ltd.
Pitfield, Milton Keynes, MK11 3LW, UK
UKHW020048311224
452994UK00004B/398